Dedication

This book is dedicated to the Baby Boomer generation. We worked hard and played hard. Now as retirement looms, many of us have found our savings and assets decimated by the Great Recession. But we will overcome this setback too. The spirit of our generation does not know how to give up. We will find a way to continue our contribution to society and the next generation.

Table of Contents

Chapter 1 - Introduction.. **1**

What is the Purpose of this Book? 2

Who will this Book Help?... 2

A Word about your Retirement Perspective 3

Factoids – Retiring Baby Boomers....................................... 5

Chapter 2 – What Does Your Retirement Look Like? **8**

Eureka!.. 9

Chapter 3 - What Savings and Income will be Available to You during Retirement? **11**

Let's "Ballpark" your Retirement Savings and Income 11

Chapter 4 – Your Current Situation and Social Security **15**

Will Social Security Still be Around When I Retire?................................. 16

How are Social Security Benefits Computed? 16

Spousal Benefits.. 17

What Happens if a Spouse Dies? 17

Divorced? You May be Entitled to Receive Benefits Based on your Ex's Earnings 17

When should I Begin to Take Social Security Benefits?........................... 18

If You Work, Watch out for Earning Limits before Reaching Full Retirement Age 18

Collecting Unemployment? 19

Social Security Benefits are Protected under Bankruptcy 19

Some Strategies to Consider 20

Work Longer to Increase your Benefits 20

Delay Applying for Benefits as Long as Possible 21

Take your Social Security Benefits Early to Avoid Tapping into Retirement Investments 21

Let the Low-Earning Spouse Claim Benefits First 21

If You are Single, Claim your Benefits Earlier 21

My Thoughts 21

Chapter 5 – Medicare and You 23

What is Medicare? 23

Long-Term Care 24

Chapter 6 – Boomer Veterans Benefits 27

Home Purchase 27

Life Insurance 28

Healthcare 28

Assisted Living and Long-Term Care 29

Burial Expenses 29

Small Business Administration Special Assistance 30

Education Assistance 30

Chapter 7 – Recommendations for Boomers in Their 50's 31

Continue to Work 31

Work a Second Job 31

Cut your Spending and Pour More into Savings 31

Pay Off Credit Cards and Other Debts 32

If You are Not Working 32

Invest More Aggressively 32

Take Advantage of Today's Low Real Estate Prices and Interest Rates ... 32

Delay Taking Social Security Benefits as Long as Possible 32

Chapter 8 – Supplementing your Retirement Income 34

Start a Home-Based Business 34

Prepare a Business Plan First! 35

Be Cautious About Pitched Opportunities 36

Protect your Assets 37

Launch an Internet-Based Business 37

Recommended Easy Website Development Tools 38

Where can I Find Home-Based Business Opportunities and Ideas?.........39

Select a Multi-Level Marketing Business...40

Where can I find MLM Opportunities?..41

Work Part-Time 42

Chapter 9 – What Should You Do with your Current Home?...........45

If You Intend to Stay in your Home...45

Refinance to Take Advantage of Today's Low Rates..............................45

Is a Reverse Mortgage Right for You? 46

Is your Home Equity Underwater?..47

Selling your Home? Optimize your Return with Carry-Back Financing......50

Chapter 10 – Reduce Expenses by Relocating to a Less Expensive Area or Exploring Alternative Housing 55

Reduce Expenses by Moving to a less Expensive Location......................55

Location is Important!...56

Housing Alternatives for Baby Boomers 56

Downsize for Boomer Retirement...56

Mobile Home Communities for Boomer Retirement 57

Co-Housing for Low-Cost Retirement 58

Shared Housing 59

Retirement and Assisted-Living Communities..........................59

Rural Areas Offer Home Financing for Low-Income Baby Boomers!...59

Housing Assistance..60

Area Affordability Index 60

Most Affordable Cities 61

Most Affordable Cities to Buy a House 61

Chapter 11 – Stretch your Dollars by Retiring Abroad 63

Argentina...65

Belize..66

Brazil 66

Chile 66

Costa Rica..66

Dominican Republic 67

Ecuador 67

El Salvador...67

Mexico..68

Nicaragua 68

Panama 68

Peru 69

Puerto Rico..69

Uruguay 69

Chapter 12 – Reducing Everyday Expenses without Sacrificing your Lifestyle Quality...**70**

Revamp your Phone Service 70

Cut Utility Costs 71

Clip Coupons and Shop Sales..................................72

Reduce your Home Entertainment Costs..................73

    Downloading TV Shows and Movies........................74

    TV-Internet Boxes...75

    Satellite TV Services 76

    FREE Movies 77

    Cheap DVD Rentals 77

Cut Back on "Nice to Haves" 77

Trim Insurance Costs 78

Perform Common Household Repairs and Upgrades Yourself 78

Reduce Car Expenses 78

Replacing your Car...79

Cut your Pet Care Costs..79

Chapter 13 - Take Advantage of Inexpensive Travel........................**81**

Inexpensive Domestic Travel..81

Low-Cost Local Vacations...81

Low Cost Airfare..81

Traveling Abroad on a Budget 82

Affordable Baby Boomer Cruises...82

Join Clubs 82

Chapter 14 —Reducing Healthcare Costs for Those Under 65 83

Shop Health Insurance 83

Discount Healthcare..85

Cutting your Prescription Costs...85

Low-Cost Dental Plans 86

Discount Vision Care...87

Chapter 15 – Handling Parental Care Issues and Expenses............ 88

Chapter 16 – Real World Examples 91

Example 1 – Older Boomer Loses Job 91

Example 2 – Boomers Forced into Retirement with Little Savings 92

Example 3 – Boomers Retiring on a Low Income after Losing their Home and Savings.. 94

Example 4 – Retiring Boomers Need to Supplement their Income.......... 95

Example 5 – Make Lemonade Out of Lemons! 96

Chapter 17 — Now it is Up to You! 98

Chapter 18 — My Story 101

About the Author 103

Chapter 1 - Introduction

If you were born between 1946 and 1964, you are a Baby Boomer. I am a Baby Boomer myself. The older members of our generation (like me) are now reaching age 65 at the rate of 10,000 daily in the U.S, continuing for the next 19 years. Many of us are unprepared financially for retirement, yet here we are.

Financial surveys have shown that roughly half of Boomers above the age of fifty have insufficient financial resources to retire in the life style they had envisioned. Many have only a portion of the assets financial planners say they will need to sustain twenty or thirty years of retirement. Some have no assets at all except for the expectation of social security or receiving a pension.

Older Boomers have been hit especially hard by the Great Recession. For many, half or more of our lifetime savings invested in 401Ks disappeared before we managed to stop the bleeding. Most of us were depending on our home equity to fund a large portion of our retirement, but that evaporated and many Boomers are now upside-down on their mortgages. Many more have lost their homes and fear a bleak future. The worst thing is that older Boomers do not have time to make up these losses before age and industry force retirement upon them.

We're angry and scared. We did everything right, yet the economic rug was pulled out from under us. Our retirement plans have been vaporized and the future looks dim. All this while those who were responsible for the Great Recession seem to prosper and continue on their way with outrageous bonuses. The game seems rigged against older Boomers, and no one is going to bail us out. The Government is focused on salvaging the "too big to fail" banking and financial industries. Having digested our bail-out funds, Wall Street has gone on its merry way, strangely devoid from what is happening on main street America. Outside of AARP, no one seems concerned with the plight of older Baby Boomers hammered by the Great Recession. No agency is going to compensate Boomers for their losses. Older Baby Boomers are entirely on their own and can expect no sympathy or special assistance.

So, are we just out of luck? Are we destined to live the rest of lives in poverty or working until we're eighty as greeters at discount retail outlets? Is that our future?

NO! Practically anyone who has some form of income can enjoy a relatively "comfortable" retirement and this book will show you how. Our generation changed the world, fought a brutal war in Vietnam, raised families, powered America's businesses to new heights, created world-changing technologies and played hard along the way. But one thing we never did was to give or fall victim to despair.

What is the Purpose of this Book?

If you are one of the fortunate Boomers unaffected by the Great Recession or who has a large retirement fund or inheritance, this book may not be for you. For the rest of you, it may be the answer to your prayers.

This book is actually a survival guide for shell-shocked Boomers whose life savings and retirement plans have been devastated by the Great Recession. It will also help those who lived large on good incomes without giving too much thought to retirement and now see financial reality staring them in the face. Younger Boomers who are worried about the future will walk away realizing that there are always retirement options if you are prepared to expand your horizons.

Here you will find the results of in-depth research consuming thousands of hours into hundreds of online resources. This guide also reflects the real life experiences of countless Boomers overcoming financial hardships through innovative strategies to keep their retirement dreams alive. It includes the knowledge and insights gained through considerable soul searching during the middle of the night by Boomers facing desperate situations.

Who will this Book Help?

Whatever your situation, you will discover options and alternatives that open your mind to new possibilities. You will walk away with an enhanced vision of what "retirement" could mean for you. Your very concept of retirement will be expanded. Moreover, the fears and anxiety that creep into your mind about retirement will be replaced with anticipation, excitement and a certainty that "Yes indeed," you can still take control over your destiny.

Boomers fifty and older face especially difficult challenges, and this book will help:

- Baby Boomers still in their fifties who have only limited (or no) retirement savings set aside. This book a will open your mind to new opportunities and ideas in planning your retirement.

- Older Boomers who have lost their jobs or been forced into retirement and are looking for a survival strategy. Your eyes will be opened to new ideas and resources that can help in formulating a realistic plan which addresses your unique situation.

- Boomers age sixty-plus who lost a good portion or all of their financial nest egg during the Great Recession. You will learn how to stretch your remaining dollars so that you can still spend your retirement in a comfortable fashion. In short, you will expand your options and see how to make the most with your remaining assets and income.

The knowledge encapsulated within these pages is for older Boomers who are financially struggling and wondering how they can ever escape the grind of daily employment or survive in today's economy now that their job has disappeared.

But as a last word, I suggest that even those who have escaped the recession with retirement funds intact may benefit from the alternatives discussed herein. It all depends on what you intend to do during your retirement years, whether you plan to remain actively engaged in social and business issues or intend to focus on a life of leisure. Even if you are not financially challenged during retirement, the information and knowledge presented here will broaden your perspective and insight. You can also gain a better understanding of what the majority of Boomers are enduring and how their determination and creativity is leading them to overcome adversities to achieve rewarding retirements.

A Word about your Retirement Perspective

Everyone harbors a vision about their personal retirement. Maybe you envision a life of luxury, or starting a second career based on what you really want to do. Perhaps you have dreamed of cruising around the world for a year, exploring major cities and historical sites along the way. Or maybe you want to perform volunteer work to give something back to society. Some will go back to school or start their own business. We all have a retirement dream.

Based on the retirement assets you have left, that vision will have to be adapted to today's reality. It is likely that you have fewer chestnuts in your nest egg than planned. Wishing aside, that is what you have to work with…and you must modify your retirement strategy to fit reality. Your retirement may have to be downsized or simply approached in a different fashion. You should also be open to new possibilities. In the end, you will discover there is more than one way to achieve your retirement goals.

As you approach your retirement planning, it is beneficial to re-examine your priorities. For example, using Maslow's hierarchy of needs, it should be obvious that having a secure roof over your head during retirement is a high priority. Maybe driving the latest SUV model or traveling the globe is not. Some things are nice to have while others are essential.

Most of you have labored for thirty or so years by the time retirement age comes. Stop and think – isn't being the master of your own time the most important thing in the autumn and winter of your life? Remember those really nice days when you thought, "I wish I could take the day off and go to the beach or the park?" Well, retirement affords that. It gives you the freedom to focus your time and energies on things you – not your boss or others - consider important. Every morning when you wake up, you will control how your day is spent.

It is likely that the scope of your original retirement dream is no longer realistic. However, if controlling your own time and how it is spent is your top priority, this is achievable. You will discover that you can still enjoy a fulfilling and stimulating retirement regardless of your current financial situation.

But you have to be willing to throw out preconceptions and build a new retirement plan that is in synch with anticipated financial resources. To be successful, you must play the cards you have been dealt.

Most Boomers do not envision "retirement" being nothing but sitting around, playing golf, going to parties or generally living a "summer vacation" life. Sure, there's some of that, but surveys show that most Boomers intend to stay involved through volunteering or starting a home-based business. A large number intend to postpone retirement until their seventies, either because they enjoy their work and/or because they can't afford to retire.

Whatever your situation, you can have a rewarding retirement...even if your financial capabilities are less than anticipated. You just need an open mind, awareness of the supplemental resources available to you and a willingness to embrace creative strategies...and I'm going to show you how.

Factoids – Retiring Baby Boomers

- The collapse of the housing bubble has decimated the holdings of the vast majority of near retirees, who will have little or no housing wealth this year and will be almost totally reliant on Social Security and Medicare to support them after retirement. Source: Center for Economic and Policy Research (http://www.cepr.net)

- According to a 2011 survey by the Harris Poll, among Baby Boomers ages 46 to 64, 25 percent have no retirement savings. And among mature Boomers, those ages 65 and over, 22 percent have no retirement savings.

- AARP surveys show that almost 90 percent of Boomers plan to work past retirement age, perhaps in part because the recession has exacted a steep toll on their pensions and savings.

- The U.S. Labor Department says layoffs have slammed workers 55 and older with record unemployment levels. Studies show that older job seekers – labeled "the new unemployables" by Boston College's Sloan Center on Aging & Work – tend to take longer to find new jobs.

- After surveying 536 U.S. employees between the ages of 60 and 65, CareerBuilder.com found that approximately 65 percent of respondents said finances are preventing them from retiring when they had planned.

- Men aged 51 to 60 are 39 percent less likely to get a job each month than younger workers. Women are 18 percent less likely to get a job. For even older workers, that number jumps to 50 percent. Source: Melissa Holmes, www.wivb.com

- Many retirees banked on their homes as their retirement fund. But the crash in housing prices has slashed almost a third of a typical home's value. Now 22 percent of homeowners, or nearly 11 million people, owe more on their mortgage than their home is worth. Many are Boomers. Nearly two in three people age 55 to 64 had a mortgage in 2007, with a median debt of $85,000. Source: Dave Carpenter, AP Personal Finance Writer

- According to the Employee Benefits Research Institute, a think tank, two-thirds of workers—and two-thirds of retirees—have saved less than $50,000 for their retirement. Half of early-cohort Baby Boomers (age 56-62) are in danger of running out of money for basic retirement expenses.

- More than other age groups, Boomers worry that their standard of living has slipped compared with that of their parents, according to the Pew study – and more than a third of Boomers fear that their kids' standard of living will be even worse.

- U.S. Baby Boomer Demographics:

  o Baby Boomers represent 26.1% of the total U.S. population.

  o 22% identify their health as "excellent."

  o 40% are overweight.

  o 51% are grandparents.

  o 48% are without a financial advisor.

  o $62,300 is the median household income.

  o 12 hours monthly are spent in volunteering.

  o Life expectancy of males is 79 and females are 83.

  o One-fifth of older workers and their spouses -- 7 million Americans -- either have no healthcare insurance or have been uninsured at some time since age 50. Source: The Commonwealth Fund.

  o There are 96.4 male Boomers for every 100 female Boomers.

  o 8.9 million Boomers reside in California—the most of any state.

Sources: AARP, Census Bureau, MainStay Investments, Grandparents.com, The Wall Street Journal and FaxStoc

- Half of the Internet users aged 50-64 use social media now. The number of Facebook users in the U.S. aged 55 and older grew from around 1 million in early 2009 to about 10 million in early 2010. Source: Kaufmann Foundation.

Chapter 2 – What Does Your Retirement Look Like?

Let's start by taking a moment to describe what is important when you think of "retirement." Envision retirement in terms of the activities and experiences that give you pleasure and fulfillment instead of the material aspects making these possible. For example, buying a luxury yacht isn't necessary to enjoy the thrill of sailing.

What is important to you? What have you been yearning to do all these years? Write these thoughts down. This exercise will help you to crystallize your retirement priorities. Examples of what I usually hear from Boomers are to:

Retirement Goal	Typical Comments
Be able to manage my own time.	Freedom! The ability to plan my day according to what I want to do, to have time for relaxation every day.
Be secure and comfortable.	Ensure that I have roof over my head. Not to worry about finances. To live in a location and home that I like which is safe and feels good to me.
Spend more time with my family.	I want to do more with my wife – travel, movies, dinners, walks – and spend time with the grandkids.
Give something back.	I want to volunteer for a worthy cause, such as helping under-privileged kids with their reading, serving in my church, get elected to the city council, or serve on my HOA Board.
Start a business based on a hobby or one that leverages my experience and skills.	I want to be my own boss, to work full-time or part-time as it suits me. I will start a home-based business to supplement my retirement income.

Retirement Goal	Typical Comments
Travel and explore the world.	We're going to visit Europe and the Far East, maybe take a train across Australia. I want to go to museums to study art and histories.
Now that I have the time, try new things.	I'm going to take up sailing and try scuba diving. Maybe learn to fly a plane. I want to hike the Sierras. We're going to get an RV and drive across the country. I'm going to learn a new language.
Exercise every day to build energy and maintain my health.	I will go to the gym daily or take long walks. I'm going to play golf three times weekly. We intend to start our day by taking a bicycle ride every morning.

Notice that these goals are organic in nature. I have never heard anyone say, "What I want to do in retirement is to buy a new car every year." It's not about having things – it's about how you intend to spend your time now that you have the freedom to control it. It's about the activities, peace of mind and interactions that will make you happy and fulfilled during your retirement.

Eureka!

Are you beginning to see where this is headed? If you can have a fulfilling retirement, it doesn't matter whether you live in a big house or an apartment. It makes no difference whether you drive a five-year-old car or a new one, if you get your books from the library or buy them new, or if you travel first-class or coach. You can get pleasurable exercise by walking or riding a bicycle just as easy as having a personal trainer. Regardless of your budget status, there are a myriad of ways to accomplish your retirement goals when viewed from the perspective of "fulfillment" rather than "lifestyle."

Now, some of you may be hung up on social status. This will be an obstacle to your happiness if your financial situation requires giving up expensive activities and possessions in order to have an enjoyable retirement. If you can spend worthwhile evenings with your family and friends having a backyard barbecue instead of dining at a five-star restaurant, is the experience any less enjoyable? If you live in a modular home in a 55+ park on an ocean bay with clean air and good friends instead of owning a villa, is your life less fulfilling? Let go of debilitating social perceptions. Learn instead to focus on having quality experiences, good friends and spiritual peace in your heart. You will be a lot happier in the fall and winter of your life.

Once you perceive your retirement in terms of fulfillment rather than a need to live at a certain monetary level or maintain a social image, the opportunities for happiness within your financial means explode. An exciting, rewarding retirement is within your grasp. The quality of your retirement years has nothing to do with how much money you have. "Retirement" is a state of mind and your expectations. Regardless of how skinny your savings account is, you can still have a quality retirement based on the activities, people and love you bring into your life. Peace of mind and good cheer come from within your soul, and are not dependent on the size of your pocketbook or the lifestyle you live. Achieve this perspective and your retirement, whatever form it may take, will bring you fulfillment and many years of happiness, adventure and inner peace.

Chapter 3 - What Savings and Income will be Available to You during Retirement?

This book is designed to open your eyes to new resources and ways of achieving your retirement dream no matter what your financial situation. I define "retirement" as doing what you want to do, enjoying a comfortable lifestyle achievable within your financial means. I am going to expand your horizons, demonstrating how your retirement goals are still feasible even with diminished assets.

So let's begin your retirement journey by determining what assets you have to work with. This is a necessary exercise to quantify your retirement income and savings. It is the prism through which you will filter possible retirement scenarios to determine what is financially feasible. The reality of your financial profile governs how you can achieve your retirement objectives.

I'm not talking about an in-depth financial analysis – that is something you can do later – but an "off the top of your head" and "check your statement"-type summary. We're looking for a ballpark assessment of the funds and income you expect to have available upon retirement.

This information is important because it helps to focus your retirement plans. Once you know what funds are available to work with, you have a perspective for evaluating feasible retirement alternatives. It will help you to separate "what is possible" from "wouldn't it be nice if…" Then you can begin to refine your retirement plans and focus on strategies compatible with your financial means.

Let's "Ballpark" your Retirement Savings and Income

The form at the end of this chapter provides a means to summarize the savings and income you expect to have during retirement. Whatever your situation, your retirement lifestyle will ultimately be determined by the anticipated savings and income available to support yourself. A blank copy of this form can be safely downloaded in PDF format from the Internet by going to <u>www.BabyBoomerLifeboat.com/Resources</u>.

Rather than explain each field, a completed example is also included at the end of this chapter. The more effort you put into crystallizing your financial resources, the more confidence you will enjoy when deriving your personal retirement strategy while proceeding through this book.

You can see that this information provides a "sanity check" for assessing whether specific retirement scenarios are financially practical. It also provides a filter to screen alternative strategies for achieving your retirement dream. A realistic assessment of your expected finances allows you to set practical expectations.

Simply because you don't have the assets to pursue a retirement as originally envisioned doesn't mean your dream must be abandoned. It may still be possible when using the ideas, resources and strategies introduced within the following pages.

We will begin by gaining a better understanding of that mainstay of Boomer retirement – Social Security benefits. You may be surprised at the benefits for which you are eligible. At minimum, you will gain insight into optimizing your Social Security strategy for maximum pay-out within your circumstances.

Worksheet - Anticipated Retirement Financial Outlook		
	Amount	Comments
Savings		
Financial Investments		
Stocks		
Mutual Funds		
Bonds		
Other		
Other		
Other		
Total Investments		
Properties		
Equity #1		
Equity #2		
Equity #3		
Total Property Equities		
Total Savings		
Monthly Income		
Work		
Social Security		
Pensions		
Annuities		
Investments		
Other		
Other		
Other		
Total Monthly Income		
Notes:		

Completed Example
Worksheet - Anticipated Retirement Financial Outlook

	Amount	Comments
Savings		
Financial Investments		
Stocks	$ -	
Mutual Funds	$ 35,000	*Our 401K plans + TRowe Price personal investments*
Bonds	$ -	
Other - CDs	$ 5,000	*Chase Bank CDs maturing in 2012*
Other	$ -	
Other	$ -	
Total Investments	$ 40,000	
Properties		
Equity #1	$ 20,000	*Home equity in Grandma's house willed to us*
Equity #2		
Equity #3		
Total Property Equities		
Total Savings	$ 60,000	*Save as emergency fund.*
Monthly Income		
Work	$ -	
Social Security	$ 2,400	*Monthly benefit for Donna and I*
Pensions	$ 200	*Donna's monthly pension from Acme Corp.*
Annuities	$ -	
Investments	$ -	
Other - Home-based business	$ 500	*Start home-based business before retiring.*
Other	$ -	
Other	$ -	
Total Monthly Income	$ 3,100	

Notes: *Monthly income will increase as my home business grows. Spendable income will go up when we qualify for Medicare. Can also use emergency fund as down payment on retirement home.*

Chapter 4 – Your Current Situation and Social Security

As you read this book, are you in your fifties and employed, wondering about how you can ever retire? Perhaps you have lost your job and are beginning to realize how difficult it is today to find new employment when you are over fifty. Maybe you have a home-based business or a small company. Some of you may even already be retired.

Those of you who are – or have been – public employees, likely have a secure pension. Typically, you can also retire earlier than people in private enterprise. Social Security benefits may not apply to you unless your spouse is eligible or you have previously paid into it. For example, if you also had Social Security deductions when working a civilian job, you may be eligible for benefits – check with the Social Security Administration (SSA) regarding the "Windfall Elimination Provision."

A majority of Americans depend to some degree on Social Security to fund their retirement. Social Security is a complex subject and like a mine field, it is easy to misstep unless you are careful. My purpose here is not to describe the "ins and outs" of the Social Security program. I strongly urge readers to go to the excellent SSA website, www.ssa.gov to educate yourself about the program and get any questions answered. I want to point out a few considerations for older Baby Boomers that will impact the amount of benefits they receive.

For those eligible, you should be receiving an annual report from the SSA detailing your earnings and estimated benefits by year of retirement. If not, contact your local SSA at 1-800-772-1213 immediately or go to www.ssa.gov. You can even roughly calculate your likely monthly benefits by using a Social Security calculator provided on the site.

Another note – your Social Security "full retirement age" (when you can receive benefits, yet work as much as you want) depends upon when you were born. Boomers born between 1946 and 1954 reach full retirement at age 66. However, those born towards the end of the Baby Boomer generation (1960 - 1964) must currently wait until they are 67. Full retirement age is likely to increase over time as Congress searches for ways to reduce the national deficit, so be sure to confirm your age on the SSA website.

Will Social Security Still be Around When I Retire?

According to the Associated Press in 2011, new Congressional projections show the Social Security program running deficits every year until its trust funds are drained in approximately 2037. Waves of retiring Baby Boomers are expediting concern about the long-term financial viability of the program.

A myriad of proposals are circulating in Washington to "fix" Social Security. Only fringe groups want to completely eliminate Social Security. The most popular idea seems to be gradually increasing the eligibility age (now 62) and increasing the income ceiling under which Social Security taxes must be paid. Usually, these proposals include a "grandfather" clause for Boomers 55 and older so that they would not be affected by any changes.

It is highly unlikely that the Social Security program will be discontinued. The majority of Americans have come to depend on it for a significant portion of their retirement income. However, it will probably be modified within a few years to ensure its solvency.

How are your Social Security Benefits Computed?

The SSA computes Social Security benefits on the basis of you having worked and paid into the account for 35 years. If you don't work for 35 years, then zero dollars are assigned to each of the remaining years. Just exactly how your monthly benefits are computed is an enjoyable exercise you can accomplish by going to the SSA site. Their straightforward explanation is:

> *Many people wonder how their benefit is figured. Social Security benefits are based on your lifetime earnings. Your actual earnings are adjusted or "indexed" to account for changes in average wages since the year the earnings were received. Then Social Security calculates your average indexed monthly earnings during the 35 years in which you earned the most. We apply a formula to these earnings and arrive at your basic benefit or "primary insurance amount" (PIA). This is how much you would receive at your full retirement age—65 or older, depending on your date of birth. [For those born after 1960, the full retirement age is 67]*

All clear? Again, you should receive an annual statement from the SSA which includes an estimate of your benefits so that there are no surprises. Alternatively, you can visit your local SSA office and spend a few wonderful hours receiving an in-depth explanation. My advice - make an appointment first.

Spousal Benefits

Did you know that your wife is entitled to Social Security benefits, even if she never worked?! Yep, she (or he) can receive up to 50 percent of your monthly benefits starting at their eligibility age (now 62), regardless of whether you have elected to begin receiving your benefits.

The spouse's benefits are reduced if claimed earlier than the full retirement age. For example, a woman who claims her spouse's benefit at age 62 will receive only 35 percent of her husband's benefit, whereas she would get 50 percent by waiting until age 66 or 67. Now, if both partners in a marriage work, they can of course earn their own Social Security benefits. However, one partner still has the option of taking 50 percent of his/her spouse's benefit if the other partner earned considerably more over their working career.

What Happens if a Spouse Dies?

The surviving spouse can receive up to 100 percent of their husband's or wife's benefits. Even if deceased spouse's benefit is bigger than what they would get on their own, the surviving spouse is entitled to it. Just like normal Social Security benefit payments, the longer he/she delays claiming the benefit (up to age 70), the more money they will receive. And even if a surviving spouse receives the deceased benefits, they also remain eligible to receive their own earned benefits provided they have paid Social security taxes over the years.

Divorced? You May be Entitled to Receive Benefits Based on your Ex's Earnings

If you are divorced and single, you could be entitled to more Social Security benefits based on your ex's earnings. Assuming you were the low-earner and your marriage lasted at least ten years, then you are entitled to a monthly amount equal to 50 percent of your ex's benefits, starting when you reach the age 62. This has no effect on your ex's benefits. And after your ex dies, you are eligible for "survivor's benefits" which are equal to 100 percent of what your ex was receiving!

The catch is, you can't receive both your ex's and your benefits – you have to choose one or the other. So, this only makes sense if your ex's benefits are larger than those you would receive based on your own earnings. If your ex is still alive, then 50 percent of his benefits must be bigger than 100 percent of yours for this to make sense. When he/she dies, you can elect to switch over if all of your ex's monthly benefits are larger than you receive on your own. Moreover, re-marriage after the age 60 means you can still claim survivor's benefits if your ex has expired. Source: Barbara Shapiro, Certified Divorce Financial Analyst (www.bshapiro-cdfa.com)

When should I Begin to Take Social Security Benefits?

Currently, Baby Boomers become eligible for Social Security benefits at age 62. The major question you have to answer is "Should I sign up now for my benefits or wait until my full retirement age to get a bigger monthly check?" The answer is, "It depends." Generally speaking, retiring at age 62 will yield a monthly check that is about 70-75 percent of what it would be if you waited until your full retirement age, 66-70 years old.

Let's say your full retirement age is 66 and your monthly benefit starting at that age is $1,000. If you choose to start getting benefits at age 62, your monthly benefit will be reduced by 25 percent to $750 to account for the longer period of time you receive benefits. This is generally a permanent reduction in your monthly benefit.

If you choose to not receive benefits until age 70, you would increase your monthly benefit amount to $1,320. This increase is from delayed retirement credits you get by postponing receiving benefits past your full retirement age. The benefit amount at age 70 in this example is 32 percent more than you would receive per month if you chose to start getting benefits at full retirement age.

Another note, each year your benefits will normally be adjusted upward by a SSA "cost of living" adjustment (COLA), usually in the neighborhood of 2-3 percent. However, for 2010 and 2011 fiscal years, this has not been the case. Apparently, their inflation index does not include increased cost of energy or food!

If You Work, Watch out for Earning Limits before Reaching Full Retirement Age

If you are earning income, taking Social Security benefits and have not yet reached your age of full retirement (66 or 67), then the SSA places limits on how much you can earn before it begins to impact your monthly benefits.

Wages, bonuses, commissions, and vacation pay all count toward the income limits, but pensions, annuities, investment income, interest, and government or military retirement benefits do not. A calculator on the SSA website can tell you how your specific earnings will affect your benefits.

Be advised, this amount changes annually depending upon your age. In 2011, for example, it is $14,160. If you are under your full retirement age, the SSA will deduct $1 from your benefit payments for every $2 you earn above this annual limit. But wait – there's more. According to the SSA:

> *In the year you reach full retirement age, we deduct $1 in benefits for every $3 you earn above a different limit, but we only count earnings before the month you reach your full retirement age. If you will reach full retirement age in 2011, the limit on your earnings for the months before full retirement age is $37,680. (If you were born in 1945 or 1946, your full retirement age is 66 years.)*

So, my friends, the goal is to avoid netting more extracurricular income than the SSA annual limit. Otherwise, they will reduce your monthly benefits for the following year (based on your previous year's tax return). Operating your own business and taking full advantage of legitimate tax deductions and write-offs works to the benefit of Boomers below their full retirement age. Legal deductions, such as depreciation and operating expenses, help Boomers who run home-based businesses reduce their taxable net income, the figure reviewed by the SSA.

Collecting Unemployment?

Did you know that you can receive Social Security benefits and unemployment compensation at the same time? And that unemployment benefits are exempt from the SSA's earnings limit? The only hitch is that your unemployment benefits could be cut based on income from Social Security and other sources. It's best to check with your state unemployment office for details.

Social Security Benefits are Protected under Bankruptcy

Your Social Security benefits are protected in the event you file bankruptcy. For example, they are not included in the calculation of disposable income when setting up a debtor repayment plan under Chapter 13 bankruptcy.

Some Strategies to Consider

Like taxes, people have learned to "game" the Social Security system, figuring out ways to maximize benefits pay-out or how to optimize retirement economics when Social Security benefits are part of the mix. Some of these strategies are presented here for your consideration.

These are not recommendations. Given your unique circumstances, you must decide for yourself whether there is a benefit to adopting any particular strategy. In any case, I suggest you research each strategy on the Internet yourself and confirm its benefits with the SSA.

Work Longer to Increase your Benefits

Paying Social Security taxes beyond 35 years has no merit. But if you have worked for, say, 30 years, it might be to your benefit to work longer just to avoid having your contribution become zero during the last five years. But working longer does not necessarily mean your benefits will be increased – it depends on the amount of your contributions over the years. Sounds strange, doesn't it? But beyond a certain point, the way SSA computes benefits means that continuing to work a few more years may have little or no increase in the amount of your monthly benefit check.

Apparently, working longer is best if you had low contributions during your early years and then higher contributions during the latter years of paying into Social Security. For example, a stay-at-home Mom who only worked as a temp during Holiday seasons, then went back to work full-time after the kids left the nest would probably enjoy larger benefits pay-out upon retirement.

Certainly, working longer has considerable benefit if you increase your 401K contributions, especially if your employer is depositing matching contributions. The higher your salary and other income benefits, the more you should be able to save during your latter employment years. It may also be beneficial if you are going to receive a pension.

Remember, if you work until age 66 or 67 before applying for your Social Security benefits, then you can continue to work if you wish (or work part-time or start a home-based business) without any income penalties! This "double dipping" aspect is especially beneficial for self-employed Baby Boomers.

Delay Applying for Benefits as Long as Possible

Every year beyond the age of 62 that you delay taking your Social Security benefits will increase your monthly pay-out by about eight percent. Claiming your benefits at age 62 results in a 25 percent lifetime decrease compared to waiting to age 70 to receive monthly payments. Generally speaking, the longer you can wait to apply for benefits, the better off you will be in the long run.

Take your Social Security Benefits Early to Avoid Tapping into Retirement Investments

If you are fortunate to have considerable investments in stocks, bonds, currencies and real estate that are delivering high returns, you may want to begin taking your Social Security benefits before your full retirement age if you need the income. This approach provides more time for your higher-earning investments to grow. However, definitely consult a financial advisor to determine the optimal course of action.

Let the Low-Earning Spouse Claim Benefits First

If you intend to continue working and earn considerably more than your spouse, letting he or she retire first may boost your combined income because the lower-earning spouse is entitled to at least 35 percent of your benefits at that point. Then, if the high-earner delays claiming benefits until full retirement age (66 or 67), both parties and the marriage optimize the total amount of benefits received. Also, if one partner dies, the surviving spouse can receive 100 percent of the high earner's benefits.

If You are Single, Claim your Benefits Earlier

Contrary to what you may believe, actuaries have demonstrated that single people do not live as long as married people. So if you are a Boomer in your sixties with no martial ties on the horizon, statistically you will able to collect more lifetime Social Security benefits by claiming them before your full retirement age (excluding any continuing work penalties, if relevant).

My Thoughts

As a Baby Boomer myself, here are my thoughts:

- If you're tired of working for someone else and need the money to get by should you quit your job, start taking Social Security payments at age 62.

- If you are 62 or older and have lost your job, your unemployment has run out and you can't find employment, start taking Social Security benefits.

- If you intend to continue working, but would like to start getting Social Security benefits before age 66, carefully investigate the net earnings limit to avoid having your monthly benefits penalized. This strategy works best for those who plan to work part-time or start a home business.

- If you are concerned that Social Security benefits will be reduced in the future, start taking payments at age 62 [Note that if no significant changes are made to the Social Security program, the Trust Funds will be exhausted by 2037 and Social Security will be unable to meet all of its benefit obligations.]

- If you have health problems, start taking payments at age 62.

- If you plan to continue working and are pulling in more than $1,000 monthly, delay taking Social Security benefits as long as you can. This will boost your monthly benefits payment.

- Generally speaking, the longer you can put off receiving Social Security benefits, the higher your monthly benefits check will be.

- Always arrange direct deposit to a bank account to prevent theft of your Social Security check!

Chapter 5 – Medicare and You

Healthcare insurance is a major expense for Boomers who are over 50 but not yet 65. I know that for my wife and me, a simple catastrophic medical policy cost us $800 monthly. And we are both in good health, taking only one or two minor prescriptions. This policy had high co-pays and only provided minimal prescription coverage. Every time I cut back on coverage in an attempt to make premiums more affordable, the insurance company inevitability raised their rates, especially as we approached retirement age.

So when I finally turned 65 and automatically qualified for Medicare, it was a nice payday! Later that year, when my wife qualified, our discretionary income jumped again. We went from $800 monthly premiums to just a total of $222 with an AARP-endorsed supplemental policy. We added optional vision, dental and hearing insurance, which we didn't have before, for another $39 each. Our co-pays are low and prescription coverage is almost 100 percent.

For the typical Baby Boomer, finally getting Medicare is like winning the lottery. This is going to save you a lot of money. It is a major factor in developing your personal survival plan for retirement.

What is Medicare?

Medicare is the U.S. government sponsored medical coverage for seniors (ages 65 and older). If you qualify for Social Security, you are automatically enrolled at age 65 and must take action if you do not want to be enrolled. If you are receiving Social Security benefits, the Medicare premiums will be automatically deducted from your monthly benefits.

A short definition of Medicare is "Medicare is health insurance for people 65 years or older, under age 65 with certain disabilities, and any age with end-stage renal disease (ESRD) or Lou Gehrig's disease. Medicare has four parts -- Part A, which is hospital insurance, Part B, which is medical insurance, Part C, which is Medicare Advantage Plans, and Part D, which is Prescription Drug Coverage." Source: www.medicare.gov

Most people elect to enroll in a Medicare Advantage Plan offered by private insurers. These replace Medicare Parts A and B with commercial coverage offering superior benefits at no additional cost. For example, AARP offers MedicareComplete from Secure Horizons through UnitedHealthcare Insurance.

To learn more about Medicare, visit their official site at www.medicare.com or AARP at www.aarp.com.

Long-Term Care

As Boomers, we can expect to live longer than previous generations. But with longevity comes the issue of illnesses associated with old age. Some studies estimate that one in four Boomers will develop Alzheimer's disease. Extended nursing home or at-home care is costly. Having sufficient funds for long-term medical care is something that most Boomers lack.

According to Medicare:

- Traditional nursing homes are facilities that provide long-term custodial care to people who cannot be cared for comfortably and/or easily at home. This can be due to physical, emotional, or mental problems. Assistance often includes help with bathing, dressing, eating, using the bathroom, and other daily activities. Payment for these types of nursing homes is not included in Medicare coverage.

- Most Medicare Part C plans, also known as Medicare Advantage Plans, provide Medicare coverage for skilled nursing facility care if the care is medically necessary. Costs and benefits may be different under different Medicare policies, including between Medicare Part C plans and Original Medicare plans. Like Original Medicare, most of these plans will not cover custodial care in nursing homes if it is the only type of care you need. However, there may be some that offer additional benefits or services. For more information, compare Medicare Advantage Plans online or contact your Medicare Part C plan provider directly.

- You can pay for nursing homes that provide custodial care with Medicaid, personal savings, a managed care plan, Medigap policies, and long-term care insurance. However, nursing homes must be under contract with a managed care plan in order for the plan to cover care. Medigap policies will only provide Medicare coverage for skilled nursing care that is covered under regular Medicare policies. This means that Medigap policies likely will not cover long-term custodial care.

- The likelihood of Baby Boomers needing some kind of long-term care is great, whether it be assisted living or skilled nursing care. This can bankrupt you. Medicare only covers so many days of long-term care before the costs start coming out of your pocket. For example, a typical Medicare supplemental or Advantage program covers the first 20 days or so of costs at a skilled nursing facility. Then for days 21-100, your co-pay is $50 daily. Thereafter, you are responsible for all ongoing costs which can reach several thousand dollars monthly.

  o The average costs in the United States (in 2009) are:

  o $198/day for a semi-private room in a nursing home ($72,270 annually)

  o $219/day for a private room in a nursing home ($79,935 annually)

  o $3,131/month for care in an Assisted Living Facility (for a one-bedroom unit)

  o $21/hour for a Home Health Aide

  o $19/hour for a Homemaker services

  o $67/day for care in an Adult Day Health Care Center

  Source: www.longtermcare.gov

Private long-term care insurance is available, but it is expensive. A 55-year-old couple now buying three years of $150-a-day coverage that adjusts with inflation might pay $2,860 a year for a policy that cost $2,200 in 2005 (http://money.cnn.com). But rates are expected to climb sharply as Boomers retire and age. The question is, will you be able to afford annual rates of say, $4,000 - $6,000 a few years from now?

Another downside of long-term care insurance is that there is no guarantee that the selected insurance company will still be in business should it become necessary to utilize the policy at a future time.

Medicaid is a state-run program for financial assistance for long-term care (see www.cms.gov/home/medicaid.asp). It can offer some assistance if your spouse requires nursing home care once your Medicare coverage is depleted, but there are "gotchas." For example, you may have to spend down your retirement assets on nursing home coverage to a certain level before you qualify for Medicaid.

So what's the bottom line? Unless you have a ton of money, few can afford long-term care! If this is a major concern for you and you are reading this book, contact Medicare and your state Medicaid program to assess your personal situation. Veterans have some other options (see the next chapter). There are also private consultants that may be able to help you minimize the impact to your finances should your spouse require long-term nursing home care (like forever).

Lacking the money to cover the costs of extended long-term care is probably not something you can do anything about. Most Boomers don't have the money to cover large private insurance premiums that grow each year. So my advice is to take legal measures to protect your assets as best you can and resign yourself to the rest being consumed before you can qualify for state assistance. It's a sad outlook, but there it is.

Affordable extended long-term care is lacking in this country. It is a recognized short-fall of national health care plans in the midst of an aging population. Some companies are experimenting with life-insurance policies or annuities that double as vehicles to cover nursing home and home-care expenses. Hopefully, some sort of national program or affordable solutions will emerge in the coming years to protect Boomers from financial ruin should they or a spouse require extended long-term care.

Another means of reducing medical expenses is using your VA benefits if you are a veteran. Military veterans also enjoy other benefits which can reduce expenses during retirement and sometimes increase their income. We will explore these topics in the next chapter.

Chapter 6 – Boomer Veterans Benefits

There are over 23 million military veterans in the United States today. Only 8 million are receiving VA benefits. If you are a veteran, your military service may qualify you to receive supplemental retirement income or provide means to reduce your living expenses.

Many of our generation got a free ticket to that vacation spot of the orient, Vietnam. Others provided support functions in nearby countries. Some served in the U.S. It makes no difference where you served – if you were in the military during a wartime period and received an honorable discharge; you are eligible for benefits from a grateful nation. Every Boomer veteran should visit the Veterans Administration website (http://www.vba.va.gov/VBA/) to ascertain what benefits may apply to their situation.

Home Purchase

Perhaps the best known VA benefit is the ability to buy a home with no money down. But maybe you didn't know that as a veteran, you can use this benefit over and over again, as long as the previous home loan was paid off.

This benefit is a bonanza for Boomer vets seeking to downsize or move for economic reasons and buy a retirement home. Provided your income qualifies – and the VA is a little more lenient than other lenders – using a VA loan can ensure that you have a roof over your head in old age even if your retirement income is less than expected. For more information, visit http://www.benefits.va.gov/homeloans/, contact a local lender or find a nearby mortgage broker who specializes in VA loans.

Some states, such as California (http://www.cdva.ca.gov/newhome.aspx) also offer veterans loans for home purchase. Some of these are "sales contracts" wherein the state actually owns the property until it is fully paid. Nonetheless, these programs can ensure that you have an affordable home in your retirement years.

Too, if you already have a VA loan, but are having trouble making your payments in these difficult economic times, the VA may be able to help you. Go to http://www.benefits.va.gov/homeloans/ for details.

The U.S. Department of Agriculture (USDA) provides loans and guarantees to buy, improve or operate farms. Loans and guarantees are generally available for housing in towns with a population up to 20,000. Applications from veterans have preference. Go to http://www.rurdev.usda.gov/Home.html for more information.

Life Insurance

Unless you are disabled from your military service, the VA does not provide life insurance for veterans of the Baby Boomer generation. However, several private insurers focus on the veteran market and offer term life insurance at favorable rates. This may be able to save you money in premiums. Two insurers to review are USAA (www.usaa.com) and the Military Benefit Association (www.militarybenefit.org).

Healthcare

All veterans qualify to some degree for free healthcare from the VA. Obviously, if you are disabled from a wartime injury, illness or trauma, you have priority in receiving healthcare. But did you know that if you served in Vietnam, you are automatically eligible for certain health benefits presumed to be associated with the chemical defoliant, Agent Orange?

On October 13, 2009, the Secretary of Veterans Affairs announced three new "presumptive" Agent Orange Conditions: Parkinson's disease, Ischemic heart disease, and B cell leukemias (including hairy cell leukemia). Tactical herbicide exposure is presumed for Veterans with service on the ground in Vietnam, or on its inland waterways. So if you served in Vietnam and suffer from one of these diseases, you are automatically eligible for VA benefits.

Veterans are also eligible for mental health benefits. Simply go to http://www.mentalhealth.va.gov/VAMentalHealthGroup.asp to learn more.

Overall, veteran healthcare benefits have expanded in recent years. This can be especially beneficial to Boomer vets in their fifties and early sixties who are not yet eligible for Medicare. Learn more at www.va.gov.

Assisted Living and Long-Term Care

Another area where your veteran's benefits may help is with assisted living, for yourself or an aging parent. Ever hear of the Veterans Aid and Attendance Pension? Thought not. It is an obscure benefit that few eligible vets have heard of.

The Veterans Aid and Attendance Pension is designed to be a safety net for any vet 65 and older. First, did you know that the VA classifies vets who are 65 or older as "disabled" regardless of their physical state? According to VeteransAid.org (www.veteransaid.org):

> *The classification of "disabled" entitles the veteran or widow for a Basic Pension if he/she meets the net worth and income criteria. The same is true for the surviving spouse. No Physician's Statement is required for filing for Basic Pension.*

To be eligible for Basic Pension in 2011:

- A veteran alone must have countable income LESS than $11,830 a year.

- A veteran with a spouse must have countable income LESS than: $15,493 a year.

- A vet can get up to $1,632 monthly; a surviving spouse is eligible for up to $1,055 monthly. A couple is entitled to receive up to $1,949 monthly.

Obviously, this benefit is designed primarily for very low-income or homeless veterans and their families. But if you have an aging parent who is a veteran living on a low-income (or perhaps living with you and just collecting Social Security or a small pension), this benefit could be a BIG help.

Finally, the government runs two retirement homes just for disabled veterans. Call 1-800-332-3527, 1-800-422-9988, or go to their website (www.afrh.gov/) for more information.

Burial Expenses

Eligible veterans and their families can get assistance with burial expenses. Veterans or their survivors are entitled to a free inscribed headstone or marker for their grave at any cemetery. Upon the veteran's death, a one-time payment of $255 also may be made to the veteran's spouse or child by the Social Security Administration.

Burial in a VA national cemetery is available for eligible Veterans, their spouses and dependents at no cost to the family and includes the gravesite, grave-liner, opening and closing of the grave, a headstone or marker, and perpetual care as part of a national shrine. For Veterans, benefits also include a burial flag and military funeral honors. Visit www.cem.va.gov to determine if a particular cemetery is open for new burials, and which other options are available.

Small Business Administration Special Assistance

Veterans interested in entrepreneurship and small business ownership should explore the U.S. Small Business Administration's (SBA) Office of Veterans Business Development (www.sba.gov/vets) for assistance. SBA is the primary federal agency responsible for assisting veterans who own or are considering starting their own small business.

SBA manages a range of special small business lending programs at thousands of locations, ranging from Micro Loans to venture capital and Surety Bond Guarantees. Veterans also participate in all SBA federal procurement programs, including a special 3 percent federal procurement goal specifically for service-connected disabled veterans, and SBA supports veterans and others participating in international trade.

It is worth talking to the SBA if you have lost your job, are thinking of retiring, or are already retired and wish to start a home-based business or an enterprise on a larger scale. They may be able to help you out with a loan at favorable rates (better than using your credit card!) and can offer free business advice.

Education Assistance

It is doubtful that any Baby Boomers will still qualify under the "GI bill" for post-service education benefits, as they must be used within ten years of leaving active duty. Nonetheless, while it was there, the GI bill helped many of us get college degrees, accomplish post-graduate work, or complete technical courses. We were grateful to have it.

Chapter 7 – Recommendations for Boomers in Their 50's

If you are in your fifties and still working, you have an opportunity to prepare for retirement. This is true even if your savings and home equity suffered during the Great Recession. I'm not saying you can get back to where you were, but you can take steps to better position yourself for comfortably retiring on a down-sized income. Here are some strategies to consider:

Continue to Work

The longer you can continue to work, the better. This is especially true if you earn more pension benefits by working longer or your employer adds matching funds for 401K contributions. And by working longer, you also have an opportunity to boost the portion of your salary or income that goes into retirement savings.

Continuing to work will also save you money on healthcare premiums, which are considerable until you qualify for Medicare. As you near retirement age, you may be able to negotiate part-time work without sacrificing medical benefits.

Work a Second Job

If possible, consider working a second job, with earnings devoted strictly to increasing your retirement savings. Every dollar added will be appreciated down the road. If you can add a few hundred dollars to your monthly retirement income, it is worth the sacrifice.

Cut your Spending and Pour More into Savings

Cutting back on spending is not as difficult as you think. Mostly, it is a matter of breaking bad habits. For example, skip Starbucks coffee in favor of less-expensive alternatives. Eat out less. Postpone buying a new car. Cut back on entertainment. Trim cable and cell charges. Consider becoming a one-car family or using public transportation more. Once you put your mind to it, you will see ample opportunity to reduce your expenses without radically impacting your lifestyle.

Take the money you save and put it into investments for retirement. You will be surprised how fast it can grow. A person age 55 who saves $300 monthly that is invested with an annual return of four percent will have an extra $44,950 upon retirement at age 65! This can boost your monthly retirement income by $150 or more without touching the principal.

Pay Off Credit Cards and Other Debts

Entering retirement with credit card or other debt is like having an anchor around your neck. Every dollar of monthly retirement income that goes towards interest payments hurts. If at all possible, get rid of financial encumbrances like these before retirement. Learn to use your credit cards only for emergencies and pay them off monthly.

If You are Not Working

Consider revamping some of your major expense items. Possibly cash in a whole-life policy in favor of more affordable term life insurance. If you and your wife have excellent health, consider reducing your healthcare coverage to handle just catastrophic events or hospitalization. Up the deductible on your car insurance. Take these savings and contribute what you can to build up your retirement kitty.

Invest More Aggressively

If you are trying to make up for lost time – or the impact of the Great Recession on your savings – consider re-distributing your investment portfolio to achieve higher returns. A financial counselor can provide advice on how to best achieve your goals within acceptable risk. But increasing your annual return from four percent to (say) twelve percent makes a big difference in the growth of your retirement funds!

Take Advantage of Today's Low Real Estate Prices and Interest Rates

The Great Recession has presented an opportunity for Baby Boomers who have the financial means to secure a retirement home before retirement. There is a window of opportunity to take advantage of depressed real estate prices and record-low loan rates to acquire the retirement home of your choice in warm areas such as California, Nevada, Arizona or Florida. Some areas have seen housing prices decrease by two-thirds compared to just a few years ago. Acting now can save you thousands of dollars. Moreover, you can enjoy lower monthly payments than anticipated. In short, you have a rare opportunity to retire in a much nicer home and location than previously envisioned.

Delay Taking Social Security Benefits as Long as Possible

Unfortunately in today's harsh economy, it may not be possible for most Boomers in their sixties to employ this strategy. But if you can delay taking Social security benefits even for a year, it will make a difference in your retirement income.

The longer you can delay taking Social Security benefits, the bigger your monthly retirement check will be. Taking your benefits at age 62 results in a permanent 25 percent loss of Social Security benefits. Waiting just five more years typically adds several hundred dollars to your monthly income.

Chapter 8 – Supplementing your Retirement Income

Most Baby Boomers reading this book are searching for a means to supplement their retirement income. Maybe you feel you don't have enough income to retire in a fashion that your wish or a location of your choice. Perhaps it is by choice – there is something you always wanted to do and now you have the time to do it. Maybe it's just a matter of survival. Whatever the reason, the majority of Boomers intend to continue working during retirement, either because they enjoy it or because it is a necessity.

Some of you already have a plan and know what you want to do in retirement. Those that have the means may open a bed and breakfast inn or buy a bakery. Some of you will go back to school to train for a new profession. Others may buy a franchise. Retirees who have sufficient savings can pursue these avenues.

But the majority of Boomers – and especially older Boomers hard hit by the Great Recession – are interested in a means to boost their retirement income. There is no "slam dunk" way to generate a monthly income beyond your current retirement benefits. Whatever opportunity you pursue will take hard work to become successful. Those in their fifties and likely still working should plan ahead and get something going now so that it is already generating income by the time you retire. For others, be prepared to evaluate opportunities and dedicate money, time and energy to build a supplemental income.

Fortunately, there are several opportunities for Boomers to build ongoing revenue streams during retirement. The major ones are discussed below.

Start a Home-Based Business

Starting a home-based business is a popular choice among Boomers. With today's technology, it is a simple matter to work out of your home office. I and many others have successfully built profitable businesses while working from home while holding staff meetings at Starbucks. Typically, all you need is a good laptop computer, mobile phone, an answering service, a car and some marketing materials. It is exciting and energizing to start and run your own business.

Whatever you do, expect to work hard to achieve success. There is no silver bullet. It typically takes several months to a year or two to generate a profitable revenue stream. Meantime, you will put in many hours of sweat equity building your business. You will make mistakes, but learn from them. Much time will be spent expanding your horizons, either through Internet research, classes, networking, or trial and error. And through it all, you will celebrate your successes, discover what works and what doesn't, be totally engaged and enjoy the stimulating feeling of being alive and building your own future.

One of the great things about being your own boss is that you manage your own time. If you like to work at night in order to have free time during daylight hours, you can. Maybe you like to break your day up, work a few hours, play a few hours, and then go back to work. If there are things you need to do during the day, you can take time off and get them done. When you want to take a walk, go to lunch with someone, join friends on a bike ride, relax, or read a book, you can. You get to weigh priorities and arrange how your time is used each day. There's nothing like it!

Eventually, a successful home-based business reaches a critical mass where it becomes self-perpetuating. Then you can afford to back off without endangering revenues. You can often transition to a passive involvement, hiring someone to run the operation for you. If your business enjoys enough success, it may even be sold for a tidy profit.

Prepare a Business Plan First!

Regardless of the type or nature of the home-based business you wish to start, an essential first step is to create a business plan. This becomes the litmus test against which you gauge progress and measure success.

Identify the strengths and weaknesses you bring to your targeted market. Test your assumptions against industry figures and what potential competitors have achieved. Be sure to identify anticipated costs and perform a realistic financial analysis. The more time you spend in upfront planning, the more likely it is that you will avoid costly pitfalls and ultimately enjoy success. If it doesn't pan out on paper, it won't work in real life either.

Your business plan does not have to be a comprehensive document. Just start by inserting what information you have and then build upon it. To get a free business plan overview, go to www.BabyBoomerLifeboat.com/doc/Internet_Biz_Plan.pdf. When you feel you have enough organized data, the business plan provides an instrument that you can show to others for knowledgeable critiques. Continue refining your plan until you are confident in your assumptions, numbers and strategy.

Do not rush to market before the foundations of your business are ready. I can't tell you how many small businesses I have seen announced before they even had a mechanism in place to take orders. Or worse yet, they received orders but could not fulfill them. Too often, newly launched businesses miss opportunities because they are not ready to capitalize on them. So make sure that you are ready to go before rolling your business out. It is difficult to recover from a botched start.

The best way to announce your business is to create a step-by-step launch plan. Identify the activities that must be accomplished before you are ready to go live. Then strategize how your announcement will be handled and what marketing activities that will support it. Be poised to take advantage of any opportunities (such as interviews for local newspapers) that may result from your announcement. Prioritize launch tasks on a checklist. A smooth roll-out gives your new business a much better chance of achieving success.

Be Cautious About Pitched Opportunities

The Internet offers a plethora of opportunities for home-based businesses. If you are considering an online business and looking at turnkey offers on the Internet, be advised that there are a huge number of scams and rip-offs out there. Some appear to be designed to do nothing more than capture your email address to sell to spam sites. I recommend getting a free Google or Yahoo email address before starting your search, so any spam will wind up in an easily discarded bucket. You are also urged to check out the Better Business Bureau alerts (www.bbb.org/us/Consumer-Tips).

Be careful! There are all kinds of scams that promise a lot and deliver little. An article by Bloomberg BusinessWeek identifies *The 10 Most Common Home-Business Scams* (http://images.businessweek.com/ss/08/07/0723_scams_to_avoid/).

Protect your Assets

We live in a dangerous business environment where anyone can sue you over frivolous issues. Be forearmed - establish either a Limited Liability Corporation (LLC) or an S-Corporation to protect your personal assets. Both can be accomplished inexpensively. Don't risk your retirement nest egg to ambulance chasers (my apologies if you are an attorney).

Launch an Internet-Based Business

From consulting services to selling products online, Baby Boomers are leveraging their work and industry experience to launch online businesses that create supplemental incomes. Some examples are:

- Marketing or sales professionals becoming consultants for local small businesses.

- Sales professionals finding a commissioned position that allows them to essentially work part-time out of their home office.

- Retired police professionals setting up home-based security consulting firms.

- Retired teachers setting up part-time tutoring for students.

- People into fashion or jewelry setting up ecommerce sites to sell affiliate products online.

- Sharing knowledge and wisdom by writing ebooks that are sold online.

- Retired accountants handling the books for small businesses.

- Offering dog training services and products to your local community.

- Buying stuff at yard sales and reselling it on eBay at a mark-up.

Another approach for Baby Boomers starting a home-based business is to switch to something entirely new, something which energizes you. For example, go into real estate sales or appraisal. Both positions allow you to work out of your home according to your own schedule. Or purchase a franchise and build a successful operation out of your home office.

A host of "canned" home business solutions are offered on the Internet. Here is some sage advice when searching for "turnkey" Internet-based businesses to minimize start-up time:

- Don't just jump into something. Use the Internet to do a lot of research first. Discover what others have found to work and "not to work." Create a mini-business plan for opportunities that look good and figure out your expected return on investment.

- Never pay money upfront just to find out what the "amazing secret" to their success is! In fact, never pay money to anyone until you have thoroughly investigated the opportunity.

- Always review references and testimonials. You can enter the site or company name in Google Search to see what others are saying about them.

- Realize that simply putting up a Website (yours or a canned site) gains you nothing! The site must first be optimized for search engines, and then you have to conduct ongoing marketing activities to drive qualified Internet traffic to it.

- Remember, there is no easy way to get rich on the Internet! It takes hard work, just like any other business. Expect to spend considerable time to become successful. In addition to putting up a Website and optimizing it for search engines, marketing functions include promoting your business through an email newsletter, blog, Facebook page, press releases, speaking engagements, tradeshows and sales aids. You must set aside time and budget for continuous marketing activities. If this is not your strength, you can learn it, outsource it to an affordable marketing firm or hire an experienced virtual assistant.

Recommended Easy Website Development Tools

Unless you have experience designing websites, I recommend you look at these easy-to-use tools to launch an Internet-based business:

- Site Build It (http://retire.sitesell.com/sbsm.html) – The top ranked suite of tools for retirees wishing to start their own home-based online business. Site Build It includes not only the tools necessary to build a superb site, but also a wealth of training, marketing research and Internet promotion tools to make your site visible to your target audience. Highly recommended.

- GoDaddy.com (www.godaddy.com) – Website hosting solution with over 400 templates and web design tools. If you know how to use Microsoft Word, you can personally design a professional looking site with a dozen pages or less. Includes free email accounts and a host of sophisticated tools, such as SQL database and ecommerce solutions. I suggest hiring a professional if your site will be large or involves ecommerce. GoDaddy provides great support.

- WordPress (www.wordpress.org) – A free semantic personal publishing platform with a focus on aesthetics, web standards, and usability. Lots of free training and plug-ins. Good for blogs and smaller sites.

- Joomla (www.joomla.org) – Free website development tool with an extensive content management system, training, tools and open source support. Allows you to quickly build and modify very nice looking, highly functional websites. Best for those who have some exposure to website design.

Where can I Find Home-Based Business Opportunities and Ideas?

Here are some good articles and helpful sites to assist you in creating your own home-based business:

- Start by reading "The Top 25 Home Based Business Ideas" (http://www.allbusiness.com/specialty-businesses/home-based-business/3315-1.html) – AllBusiness.com is a good resource for those considering starting or operating a home-based business.

- Entreprenuer.com's "Home Business Ideas" is another great place to get ideas (http://www.entrepreneur.com/homebasedbiz/homebasedideas/index115320.html)Entreprenuer.com is an excellent site with extensive resources and advice for home-based business owners.

- MySmallBiz.com (www.mysmallbiz.com) is a good resource for discovering ideas and getting advice on starting a home-based business.

- BizyMoms.com (www.bizymoms.com) home business ideas for women.

You can find many more sites dedicated to home-based businesses by entering the key phrase "home-based business ideas" into Google Search.

Select a Multi-Level Marketing Business

Multi-Level Marketing (MLM) is a popular means for supplementing income among Baby Boomers entering retirement and those wishing to start a second income in anticipation of retirement.

Network marketing is simply a distribution method. MLM companies market a service or product by recruiting and compensating individuals who in turn recruit and compensate others to market, sell and distribute their wares…and so on.

If a MLM company is totally dependent upon the recruitment of down lines to maintain profitability, it is a pyramid scheme. If a MLM company does not have a high-demand product or service, it is doomed to failure. If a MLM company claims a "miracle cure," "amazing breakthrough" or "secret formulas," watch out...especially if they require an upfront investment. An excellent article for determining whether an MLM opportunity is a pyramid scheme can be found at http://www.boomer-living.com/2010/02/its-not-a-pyramid/.

A lot of MLM companies, however, are successful and do offer products and services with true value. My advice to Baby Boomers is to closely examine MLM opportunities before jumping in, especially if they are asking for an upfront investment. Also be advised that the "free" Internet sites most MLMs offer these days are practically useless for gaining online visibility. If you elect to join a MLM business, I recommend investing in your own Website, optimizing it for Internet search engines and use online marketing to build your own branding.

Before jumping into an MLM, however, I urge you to "Google" a candidate and read "the good, the bad and the ugly." Check the company out with the Better Business Bureau and other agencies. Beware of MLMs hawking products into saturated markets. The longer the company has been around, the more danger there is that it will be difficult for you to gain market share. Validate that the product or service has value unto itself - test it yourself to be sure. Confirm that pricing is not inflated to compensate for multiple distribution levels. Understand the time and training commitment to make your investment work.

MLM network marketing may be just the answer you are looking for to create a comfortable retirement. Like starting any home based business, however, you must perform upfront research to become successful and expect to work hard to grow your business. For those that pick a good MLM product or service, however, the rewards can be considerable. Good Luck!

Where can I find MLM Opportunities?

These sites are fairly impartial and good places to start your search for an MLM business opportunity that fits your needs:

- MLMReview.org (www.mlmreview.org) – Provides objective reviews and ratings of MLM opportunities.

- MLM Watch (www.mlmwatch.org) – A skeptical guide to MLM opportunities.

- Network Marketing Review (www.networkmarketingreview.net) – Good articles, reviews and ideas covering MLM opportunities.

- Ultimate MLM Reviews (www.ultimatemlmreviews.com/) – Intended to help people make solid business decisions based on factual information and not hype.

- MLM Review Kings (www.mlmreviewkings.com) – Extensive reviews of MLM opportunities and recommendations.

- Expert MLM Review (www.expertmlmreview.org) – Critical reviews of MLM opportunities and scam exposures.

- MLM Files (www.mlmfiles.com) - MLM opportunity reviews, articles and advice.

Work Part-Time

Baby Boomers who need to supplement their Social Security, pension and/or investment income should consider working part time. Others may want to work part-time just to stay active and involved. In addition to extra income, many employers offer benefit packages to older Boomers even though they are only working part time. In fact it may be worthwhile to work part time just to receive health insurance.

Baby Boomers are fortunate in that there is a building demand for experienced, reliable senior workers:

> *"Sixty-four million Boomers are poised to retire over the decade...Depending on what they do, there may not be enough younger workers with the right skills to replace them. Some labor analysts are predicting a shortage of as much as 10 million workers by the end of the decade."* Source: Senior Citizens Employment and Training (www.seniorcitizensemployment.org).

A good place for Baby Boomers to begin a search for part-time employment is at the AARP Foundation. Its Senior Employment Service Employment Program (SCSEP) helps those 55 and older to find jobs. With over 77 project sites in 22 states and Puerto Rico, SCSEP has already helped over 400,000 low-income seniors across America develop the skills and confidence they need to secure a meaningful job, increase their financial security, and help their community. To learn more, visit the AARP resource page (**www.aarp.org/work/**).

CareerBuilder.com has launched a job site for Baby Boomers, called PrimeCB.com (**www.primecb.com**). It allows you to search for both part-time and full-time positions where employers are specifically interested in older Boomers. Sign up for alerts to automatically be notified when a position that you are interested in opens up.

Baby Boomers should also visit AARP's National Employer Team, made up of independent companies that have completed AARP screening who want to recruit and keep mature workers. This highly recommended site allows you to search by employer or by industry. Learn more at **www.aarp.org./work/**.

For rewarding work in non-profit organizations addressing crucial social and environmental areas, visit Encore Careers (www.encore.org). While there, download a free Encore Guide to learn more about pursuing careers in education, health care, government and the environment.

A great site for finding local opportunities, whether full-time or part-time work, is JobsOver50 (www.jobsover50.com). This is a free web-based employment service dedicated to the 50+ job seeker.

WyzAnt (www.wyzant.com) is another good site for those seeking part-time employment. Just sign up and go through their process to become listed in a highly-visible online database.

Of course, you should also peruse more traditional job sites for part-time or full-time work opportunities:

- Monster.com (www.monster.com) – The big daddy of job sites. Post your resume and receive job alerts for designated locations.

- The Ladders (www.theladders.com) – jobs for executives used to earning $100,000 annually or more; requires a membership fee.

- Jobs.com (www.jobs.com) – Another biggie for job seekers. Register, post your resume and objectives, and get job alerts via email.

- Hound (www.hound.com) – Newer job site that is very popular. Requires subscription, but offers free trial.

- CraigsList (www.craigslist.org) – Free site; search for part-time or full-time jobs by category and location. Used by most firms to post job openings. Be careful of scammers though.

- USAJobs (www.usajobs.gov) - Official job site of the US Federal Government. It's your one-stop source for Federal jobs and employment information.

- CareerBuilder (www.careerbuilder.com) – An oldie, but goodie job site.

As you search for a part-time job, don't get discouraged. Keep your options open and weigh the benefits of each opportunity. You may wind up doing something you never considered...and thoroughly enjoying it!

Chapter 9 – What Should You Do with your Current Home?

A major issue facing most Baby Boomers coming up on retirement is "What do I do with my home?" This question seems to be at the center of everyone's quest to develop a retirement strategy. And rightly so since your home is probably your biggest asset...or obstacle.

If you have equity in your home, your choices go down one path; if you are upside-down on your mortgage, then you have a different set of challenges. No matter what your situation, you will find alternatives here that provide more options to consider.

It doesn't matter at this point whether you want to continue living in your home or relocate to another area. We'll discuss relocation possibilities in the next chapter. For now, let's focus on the options you have and how each can work to your benefit.

If You Intend to Stay in your Home

Many Boomers want to retire right where they are. They want to stay close to their family and friends. They know their local area and are comfortable with it. Moving is the last thing on their minds.

If you fall into this category, there are several actions you can take to make your retirement more financially comfortable. Even if your mortgage is fully paid, it pays to know your options.

Refinance to Take Advantage of Today's Low Rates

Boomers who want to retire in their current home have a window of opportunity to lower their monthly mortgage payments by taking advantage of today's record low interest rates. Let's look at an example:

Current Mortgage	Current Interest Rate	Monthly Principal & Interest Payment
$172,500	7.0%	$1,141
$172,500	4.8%	$896

Refinancing to a lower 4.8 percent interest rate in this case saves the homeowner $245 monthly with minimal impact on the loan amount (it is likely to increase a little due to refinancing costs).

Now, it is assumed in this example that the market value of the home is $230,000. So the loan-to-value is roughly 75 percent. This satisfies today's refinancing criteria. It is difficult to refinance unless you have at least 20 percent equity in your home.

Refinancing also gives you the option of setting up a Home Equity Line of Credit (HELOC) against which you can draw cash as needed. This allows you to buy things or pay bills at a low interest rate. It is nice to have just in case of an emergency, such as if the washer goes out or you need to replace a dying car.

Is a Reverse Mortgage Right for You?

If you are one of the fortunate Baby Boomers who have equity left in your home, perhaps you are considering a reverse mortgage as part of your retirement plan.

With a reverse mortgage, you remain the owner of the property and continue to be responsible for making mortgage and tax payments, maintaining the home, etc. What a reverse mortgage does is to allow you to tap into any home equity to receive monthly payments.

No payments are required on the reverse mortgages during your lifetime (or as long as you continue to live in the home). You can get monthly or lump sum distributions, or a combination of both. Your heirs are responsible for repaying the loan and interest when you die. If there is some equity left, they get to keep it.

Sounds good, eh? Before you run off to your nearest lender, beware that some reverse mortgages come with extraordinary fees or high interest rates. Also, some life insurance companies try to sell annuities with a reverse mortgage, which is unnecessary.

Before talking to a lender about pursuing a reverse mortgage, I strongly recommend you educate yourself. The best means to accomplish this are by reviewing the material at AARP (http://www.aarp.org/money/credit-loans-debt/reverse_mortgages/) and Reverse Mortgage Guides.org (www.reversemortgageguides.org) to gain a good understanding of the pros and cons.

Is your Home Equity Underwater?

Baby Boomer homeowners who are "upside down" on their mortgages face tough choices. Their home equity evaporated when the recession hit, and now they owe more on the property than it is worth. Perhaps they have lost their jobs too. Their savings have likely been reduced. They look around the neighborhood and see that properties similar to theirs are selling at two-thirds or even less of their mortgage amount. What action should they take? What are their alternatives?

This is not an unusual situation. The percentage of Baby Boomer homeowners who are upside down on their mortgages varies by area, but is as high as fifty percent in some locations. Moreover, millions of homeowners have lost their jobs or suffered a medical setback that has aggravated the effects of the recession.

So what choices do upside-down Baby Boomer homeowners have? Quite a few as it turns out, but all have consequences. For those who find themselves in this position, here are the major alternatives:

1. Do nothing. If you can afford it or if your loan balance is low, continue to make your house payments and hope the real estate market bounces back. Just be sure to research the expected appreciation (or further decline) in home values within your local community. Some areas in California, Nevada, Arizona and Florida, for example, may take up to ten years or more to recover home values to pre-recession levels. But if you love your home and have the financial means (or a low loan balance), this may not present a problem.

2. Rent your home out. If it can't be sold, then perhaps your local rental market will support leasing your home out for the immediate future, allowing you to rent another home somewhere else that is more affordable. If you can get rental payments on your current dwelling that cover the principal, interest, insurance and taxes, this makes sense. You may even be able to reap a profit from renting your home out.

Meanwhile, this tactic buys time to see what happens to the housing market. After six months or so, with demonstrated rental income under a written annual contract, you can usually apply for a loan to buy a new home at today's discounted value and low interest rates in a less expensive area.

3. Get a loan modification. In some cases where there are validated extenuating circumstances (job loss, illness, etc.), lenders may offer to refinance or recast your loan to reduce payments. The government encourages this through special programs, but it is voluntary for lenders to participate. It hasn't been that successful. If you want to try this, you are better off working with an experienced attorney rather than approaching the lender yourself.

4. Walk away. "Strategic defaults" are becoming more common as the effects of the recession linger. Some economists even say a "deed in lieu of" or simply mailing your house keys to the lender makes the most sense for those that are in dire financial straits or whose property is hopelessly upside down with little prospect of ever recovering its former market value. Why throw good money after bad? Just treat your home as a bad investment and take the same action big businesses and banks do – give it back to the lender! But realize that this action will negatively impact your credit and prevent you from obtaining a new home loan for up to seven years. I recommend talking to an experienced attorney before walking away from your home.

5. Let your home go into foreclosure. Actually this is a good choice for some situations. If you have lost your job and are experiencing financial difficulties, some experts advise that you stop making house payments and let your property be foreclosed. In many cases, it can take one-to-two years for the lender(s) to actually complete the foreclosure process because they already have a huge inventory of troubled properties consuming their time. Meanwhile, you live rent-free and can save up money to get back on your feet. Lenders also prefer to have the homeowner living in the property during this time so that it is maintained. Your credit score, however, is hit hard by this action and it will be 5-7 years before you can get another home loan. But if you don't have the money, who cares?! And maybe Congress or one of the major lending agencies (FHA, etc.) will institute new policies down the road that "forgive" foreclosures sooner to expedite recovery of the housing market.

Recently, Fannie Mae launched *WaysHome* (www.KnowYourOptions.com), a free interactive multi-media tool designed to educate homeowners about their options to avoid foreclosure and take informed action. It uses innovative technology to allow homeowners to put themselves in real-life situations, make informed choices and immediately see the outcomes of those actions.

6. <u>Do a short sale</u>. In this case, the lender(s) must agree to accept a lesser pay-off on the outstanding loan(s) on your property. In essence, they acknowledge that the current market value of your home is less than the amount of the loan(s) and decide to get what they can out of the deal. Lenders are becoming more amenable to short sales because it turns out to be less costly than foreclosing. And some lenders are instituting policies of responding with acceptable sale prices within 10 days of inquiry to expedite what has been a lengthy short sale process.

To be eligible for a short sale, you must convince the lender(s) that you are experiencing a "hardship." This is a verifiable event which prevents you from making your loan payments. It could be an illness, job loss, or reduced income. For those nearing retirement, lenders will sometimes accept the argument that you will have to dip into your scant retirement savings to continue making house payments. There are no set criteria – it varies by lender.

Home lender agency policies are now recognizing the need to get short-sale homeowners back into the housing market sooner, so after two years former homeowners can now apply again for home loans. But there's a catch - Since most lenders will not do a short sale if you are still making loan payments, your real estate agent or attorney will tell you to stop making payments, and thus your credit score will take a hit…which of course makes it difficult to get a new home loan.

If you have a second mortgage or home equity loan, be sure to get a written release for the unpaid balance. Otherwise, the second lender can get a deficiency judgment or sell the loan balance to a collection agency who will hound you for years. There are also reports that lenders are selling unpaid tax bills on the property to debt collectors.

Learn to fight back! Debt collectors will bend the law as far as you let them. Understand your rights (<u>www.ftc.gov</u>) and put a stop to their harassment. The law is on your side - you simply have to educate yourself to use it to your advantage.

In any case, you will owe taxes on that portion of a home equity loan not used to directly upgrade or repair your home.

7. <u>Declare bankruptcy</u>. If things have really piled on and you are in a financial mess, declaring bankruptcy is probably the best way to go. To be eligible, you must prove your inability to regain solvency without a new financial start. But bankruptcy is a much better alternative than attempting to stay afloat in an upside-down home or doing a short sale where bill collectors (and perhaps the IRS) may still pursue you afterwards.

Note that the federal government has instituted mortgage relief laws so that you don't get hit with a huge tax burden if your home goes into foreclosure or experiences a short sale. Many states have done the same for state taxes. However, these only apply to the first mortgage. Second loans (including HELOCs) present a trickier tax situation that can result in a nasty surprise once a foreclosure or short sale transaction is completed.

Each alternative requires careful research and evaluation before taking action. Boomers are encouraged to explore their options with knowledgeable real estate agents, mortgage lenders, CPAs or an attorney before doing anything. Confirm the feasible options for your unique situation and any possible ramifications. It is usually best, however, not to approach your lender(s) first, as this may set off unforeseen consequences.

Upside-down homeowners pursuing any alternative experience stress and emotional pressure. To keep your sanity, it is advisable to take a long-term perspective and formulate a "life plan" to implement after the current unpleasant situation is resolved. Getting through difficult times is easier if you have something to look forward to.

An important consideration if you are going to take any action that affects your credit rating is to ensure you have a place to live before doing so. If you intend to walk away from your upside-down home, for example, be sure to buy or rent another home before your credit gets destroyed. The same goes for other major transactions, such as buying a car on time, etc.

Selling your Home? Optimize your Return with Carry-Back Financing

If you do not have equity in your home, it will be difficult – if not impossible – to accomplish a conventional sale. Selling your home will also be a problem unless you have enough equity to cover selling costs. A short sale may be the only answer in these situations.

But if you have sufficient equity and need the money, then selling your home may be the only choice. However, if you don't need the money all at once, there is an attractive alternative.

Because of short-sighted and often punitive policies by lenders and government-backed agencies towards those who have lost their homes, the buyer pool for the real estate market keeps shrinking. But these "outcasts" denied access to traditional financing represent viable buyers for sellers willing to consider creative financing. This will lead to a surge in seller carry-back financing, especially as Baby Boomers begin to retire and want to downsize in a slow real estate market.

Whether due to a job loss or a strategic default, when someone's home goes into foreclosure the homeowner's credit file is branded with a crimson "F" and they are barred from received a standard home loan for up to seven years. The period for short sales is 2-3 years, assuming the required decimation of credit can be rebuilt within that time. Chapter 7 bankruptcy, for example, leads to 2+ year's suspension for low-down loans backed by Fannie Mae, Freddie Mac or FHA.

Now, these unfortunate souls are not deadbeats. Most are just unlucky in that they worked in a private enterprise, an arena unshielded from Depression-level unemployment and dramatic drops in incomes. So lender attitudes and industry policies preventing them from buying a home for a number of years are really akin to "kicking them while they are down."

But most will eventually recover and find employment or salvage their small business. Then they will be in the market for buying a home again. However, they quickly discover that they are shunned by the institutional lenders.

Fortunately, their predicament coincides with another phenomena - the growing number of Baby Boomers like yourself who are either voluntarily or involuntarily (because of job loss) going into retirement. A good percentage of our generation wishes to downsize to reduce their expenses in retirement, but have difficulty selling their home. You are competing with a glut of foreclosures, investment properties and short sales for a small pool of qualified buyers. Despite historically low interest rates, worries about the economy and a growing number of excluded buyers makes selling a home difficult today in many parts of the country. Often, Boomers wind up just renting their home out because they can't find a buyer.

The stars are aligning, however. Boomers and others can tap into the growing population of potential buyers who are ineligible for normal home loans by offering carry-back financing that circumvents standard lender approval criteria. Moreover, retiring Baby Boomers reap significant tax benefits from receiving payments over time instead of lump-sum profits. They can also receive a higher price or enhanced interest rate compared to current market figures. For many sellers, carry-back financing is the perfect way to supplement their retirement income with secure monthly payments at a much higher rate than that received from bonds, CDs or annuities. In the process, they will also get renters or installment buyers who are more likely to take good care of their property.

Buyers benefit too. First, they can buy a home despite being black-listed by institutional lenders. Second, they avoid many of the fees (e.g., points) that tradition lenders charge. Third, the sales cycle is expedited. Overall, it is a much better deal than pursuing a high-rate short-term or subprime loan to buy a home.

Homeowner seller financing is nothing new. There are several universally accepted types of carry-back financing. The two most popular are:

- Lease-Purchase Option: An installment sale wherein the tenant has a purchase option that can be executed under specified conditions. Typically, part of the monthly rent is applied towards the down payment. The buyer gains title to the property upon satisfying certain mutually-agreed contractual conditions.

- All-Inclusive Trust Deed (AITD): Here the homeowner "wraps" existing liens within a new loan. The seller continues to be responsible for existing loans on the property, but makes a profit override on the entire total of all loans, thereby amplifying his return. The buyer gains title to the property and makes payments to the seller who in turn pays existing lenders.

In all cases of seller financing, it is the seller who decides the credit-worthiness of prospective buyers. The seller assumes the risk normally taken by an institutional lender. Sellers can be assisted in this process by credit reports, standard disclosure forms and experienced real estate professionals. In today's economy, a recent period of income disruption and bad credit is often bookmarked by a past history of stable income and high credit scores on one end and new employment on the other. This reflects the profile of hardworking families recovering from job losses and perhaps a foreclosure or short sale. It is up to the seller to decide if he wishes to extend credit to them. To sweeten the pot, additional security such as a co-signer on the carry-back note or a lien on personal property or other real estate can also be considered.

Carry-back financing is typically secured by a trust deed or mortgage instrument on the property that allows an expedited foreclosure process to recover the seller's asset should the buyer default on payments. Pick the right buyer and creative financing like this is very secure. Worst case, the seller gets his property back to put it on the market again. And the initial deal can be structured to ensure that the seller has sufficient funds to cover costs for this contingency.

The major obstacle to seller financing has been those pesky "due on sale" clauses that most lenders slip into their loan documentation. And they interpret "sale" as any event that impacts their interest in the property (i.e., just about everything). However, in today's climate of low interest rates, defaults and slow-moving real estate, lenders are usually open to seller financing, although many will demand a quid pro quo by recasting the terms and/or interest rates on existing liens. Currently, FHA lenders are happy to just continue receiving loan payments and their HUD overseers will not usually exercise "due on sale" clauses.

Seller financing is a not a "do it yourself" undertaking. Compliance with many statutes is required and complex legalities must be addressed. Existing lender negotiations are an integral part of these transactions. Moreover, the financial aspects, risks and tax consequences must be understood and addressed.

Anyone contemplating offering seller financing should enlist a knowledgeable real estate professional to assist them. Lease-purchase installment sales and AITDs are proven processes. Realtors employ standard forms and checklists to simplify carry-back transactions, avoid pitfalls, minimize risks and ensure legal compliance. Working with a real estate agent simplifies the sale for Baby Boomers, allowing them to confidently focus on the next stage of their lives.

In summary, carry-back seller financing benefits all parties and is expected to fill the void created by strident lender policies. Those who are economically getting back on their feet represent a growing pool of eager buyers. Boomers can sell their homes quicker, plus receive a higher return on their equities while enjoying tax benefits and a supplemental income during retirement. What's not to like?!

Chapter 10 – Reduce Expenses by Relocating to a Less Expensive Area or Exploring Alternative Housing

Thus far, you have itemized your goals based on the activities you would like to define your retirement, such as traveling, volunteering or starting a second career. You have also identified the retirement assets you expect to have and learned about major government benefit programs to which you may be entitled. And you learned how to explore part-time work possibilities and home-based business opportunities to supplement your retirement income. Moreover, you now have a better understanding of how you can handle a major item integral to retirement, namely what to do with your current home.

Now that you have a good idea of how much income and benefits you can expect to enjoy during retirement, let's look at the flip side of the coin - ways to reduce your expenses. Every dollar you can save during retirement is another dollar of income. Controlling your expenses is easier than trying to generate additional income.

You may feel that reducing your expenses equates to sacrifice and living cheaply. Not so! It just means spending wisely and taking advantage of programs and promotions that save you money. It does not require drastically lowering your lifestyle to survive on less income. There may be some changes involved, but we're not talking about living in a tent or eating cat food to survive. By opening your mind to new approaches, you can easily learn how to stretch dollars during retirement and live comfortably within your means. Let's explore new ideas and programs that will broaden your perspective.

Reduce Expenses by Moving to a less Expensive Location

A major means of reducing your costs is to relocate to an area where homes are priced lower and living expenses are considerably less. This simple step can make a huge difference in the quality of your retirement life.

One of the most effective steps Baby Boomers can take to live better on a fixed income is to relocate to an area where the cost of living is less. This can result in dramatic savings without sacrificing your quality of life. In fact, in many cases the quality of life significantly improves.

Many Baby Boomers live in relatively expensive areas, like San Diego, where home prices are dramatically higher than in the rest of the nation. Some cities, such as Manhattan, have cost of living indexes two-to-three times higher than those in the mid-west or south.

Location is Important!

I suggest starting your search by identifying the aspects of your retirement location that are personally important. Are nearby medical facilities and hospitals important? What about amenities such as theaters, museums, colleges, senior facilities, parks, skiing, etc.? And don't forget climate! Use these criteria to narrow your choices to a few regions of the globe.

Once you have identified a city or area where you would like to retire, it is strongly recommended that you visit that location to validate your research. Living in an area that you really like is important to enjoying retirement. A good way to start off is to rent a home or apartment in the area of your choice while looking for a place to buy. Also, find a local Realtor with whom you are comfortable – they can help you immensely and it's a free service for buyers and renters!

Housing Alternatives for Baby Boomers

Aside from a traditional standalone residence, a condominium or a rental, a number of alternatives exist that make sense for retirees. You may not be aware of these or possess outdated information. Maybe you have a preconceived or misinformed notion of certain types of housing solutions that is working to your detriment. It pays to consider all options, so we present alternatives here for your consideration.

Downsize for Boomer Retirement

The most obvious solution for Baby Boomers to stretch their money is to downsize your living arrangements. Big homes that were purchased to raise a family eventually turn into empty nests. Downsize to a condominium, investing the balance of your equity. Or relocate to an area where housing is less expensive, again investing the balance.

Usually this strategy results in a more enjoyable and financially comfortable retirement. Even when the real estate market is in the tank, as it is now, Baby Boomers can often rent out their home for at least a break-even situation and then purchase their ideal retirement home in a location of choice. That way, Baby Boomers can take advantage of today's low prices and sell their old home in the future when the real estate market improves.

Mobile Home Communities for Boomer Retirement

Age 55+ Mobile home communities provide affordable, comfortable housing for Baby Boomers of all ages. Many are really pre-fabricated homes and consist of landscaped parks with amenities and recreation (e.g., adjacent golf courses) in temperate locations. Most are warm communities with many activities and the opportunity to meet new friends in a secure environment.

Today, most "mobile homes" are mobile in name only. Newer ones are typically a double- or triple-wide architecture offering 960 square feet and more of living space. Inside, they look and feel like new homes with all the amenities.

Typically, mobile homes in these communities reside on rented space within a managed park. Space rent (which may include trash and water) is your main expense and can be high, so be sure to shop around and look at the park's history of rental increases. Some parks also prohibit sub-leasing, which makes it difficult if you want to move somewhere else and are having trouble selling your unit. The best way to go is to purchase a mobile home whose price includes the land or which resides in a park that is subject to rent control. And the best buy is a home that is a few years old, as mobile homes tend to depreciate (depending upon the location, of course).

Renting a mobile home is an ideal solution for some. You can get a lot for your money – live in a sunny climate, enjoy adjacent recreational facilities (such as golf courses, pools, spas, clubhouses, etc.) in quiet, secure parks close to conveniences. In many areas, monthly rents start as low as $500!

Locating a mobile home park that suits your needs requires a bit of research on your part. The Internet is a great resource, especially Google Search. Just type in a search phrase like "55+ mobile home parks in [name a state or city]."

A few sites to check out are:

- Equity LifeStyle Properties (www.equitylifestyle.com) – They own and operate the highest quality portfolio of resort communities in the United States. The firm has a controlling interest in over 300 quality resorts in 28 states and British Columbia with over 110,000 sites.

- Best Guide Retirement Communities for those 55+ (www.bestguide-retirementcommunities.com) – Review more than 500 communities for active adults over 55, listed by region and then states.

- Manufactured Home Source (www.manufacturedhomesource.com) - Brings prospective buyers of manufactured homes in contact with retailers who sell homes in the area. Search by state or zip code.

The term "manufactured home" is often used synonymously with "mobile home" or "modular home." But many manufactured and modular homes reside on permanent foundations, yet cost less than standard homes because their components are pre-fabricated and assembled onsite.

Co-Housing for Low-Cost Retirement

A novel idea gaining traction among Baby Boomers is "co-housing" or "village" living, a type of collaborative housing in which residents actively participate in the operation of their own neighborhoods. Co-housing offers Boomers communities that provide social interaction and support, individual privacy, and independence.

Co-housing units in the U.S. are typically condos. Boomers can buy and sell a unit on the open market. And this solution is affordable on a beer budget. But there may be a waiting list to buy into a community. For those finished raising kids, however, this is a great way to retire while re-invigorating your social life.

There are just over 200 cohousing associations in the U.S. today. About half are complete or nearly so. The other half are in the planning or formation stages. Source: www.cohousing-communities.com.

Besides social interaction, other benefits of co-housing are financial and environmental. The cost of a home in a co-housing community ranges from $50,000 to $160,000. Typically, since the community is planned from the ground up, being "green" is important. Shared space, resources and infrastructure mean lower costs. Source: www.goodtreevillage.org.

Co-housing offers a mixture of private homes with common areas (e.g., meal halls) and neighborhood participation. It is based on a commitment to community living. Co-housing is said to be a more healthy way of living, with social ties providing medical benefits. Some sites where you can learn more about this growing trend among Boomer retirees are:

- Co-Housing Communities (www.cohousing-communities.com) – Provides a wealth of information and the ability to search for co-housing projects by state.

- Good Tree Village (www.goodtreevillage.org) – Good example and overview of co-housing in the U.S.

- Cohousing (www.cohousing.org) – Online directory with a ton of information about co-housing.

- Facebook Alternative Housing (http://www.facebook.com/pages/Alternative-housing-ideas/115946385111800) – A Facebook page dedicated to the presenting and discussing alternative housing ideas. Lots of examples.

Shared Housing

Another alternative for low-cost housing is to share a home. Having your own room in a shared home can be delightful, assuming you get along with everybody in your "extended family." Some non-profit organizations, such as "A Lelaind Community" (www.alelaindcommunity.org), offer housing at affordable rates to active adults who are 55 and older. Options include shared single family homes, cottages, studios and in-law units.

Retirement and Assisted-Living Communities

There are a variety of planned retirement communities for Baby Boomers and seniors. Many are for active lifestyles, while others offer assisted living facilities. Most cost a lot of money, but some are affordable. Type "retirement communities" into Google Search to access hundreds of retirement and assisted-living communities.

Rural Areas Offer Home Financing for Low-Income Baby Boomers!

Rural Housing Direct Loans are loans funded directly by the government. They are available for low- and very-low income Baby Boomers to obtain home ownership.
You can get 100 percent financing, including repairs and renovations or to purchase a site and install water and sewage! Mortgage payments are based on the household's adjusted income. To qualify, your income can be as high as 50-58 percent of the average median income for the area in question.

This is a good deal for Baby Boomers who have suffered financial setbacks or live solely on Social Security. Find out if you are eligible and learn more at the USDA Rural Development Website: http://eligibility.sc.egov.usda.gov/eligibility/welcomeAction.do .

Housing Assistance

Local, state and Federal government agencies offer assistance programs to help Baby Boomers whose income is an obstacle to finding good housing. HUD has several excellent programs for seniors – go to http://portal.hud.gov/hudportal/HUD?src=/topics/information_for_senior_citizens   to learn more.

Area Affordability Index

A good site to compare the cost of living between two cities is Sperling's Best Places (www.bestplaces.net). Membership is free. This helpful tool allows you to quickly determine if moving to a specific city will lower your cost of living. For example, if I'm wondering how much cheaper it might be to live in Austin, TX rather than San Diego, CA, this tool shows me that although my salary (if employed) will likely decrease, the overall cost of living will go down 20 percent. Moreover, housing is 34 percent cheaper in Austin than San Diego!

More detailed information of key consumer costs can be purchased for about $5 for each city comparison from the Council for Community and Economic Research using the ACCRA Cost of Living Index (www.coli.org).

Just selling your home and relocating to more affordable areas may allow you to buy a new home for cash and still retain a nice nest egg to supplement Social Security or pension income. If the real estate market does not justify selling your residence now, you may be able to rent or lease it out until times are better. If this is impossible, consider the alternatives previously discussed, such as short-selling your property. Just have your ducks lined up in a row so that you are settled in a new location before your credit takes a beating.

Most Affordable Cities

A Forbes study (www.forbes.com) completed in January 2011 found the most affordable cities in terms of housing cost, amenities and employment levels are typically in the midwest. Omaha is number 1. Other heartland cities include Indianapolis, Ind. (No.4); Minneapolis-St. Paul, Minn. (No. 7); Oklahoma's namesake city (No. 9) and Tulsa (No. 15); and Ohio's three largest metros, Cincinnati (No. 5), Cleveland (No. 8) and Columbus (No. 13).

There are still places right here in the U.S. that are excellent retirement locations for Baby Boomers who must live off Social Security or a pension and have an additional small nest egg (401K, investments, etc.). Obviously, you want to avoid areas with high housing costs or which are dependent upon expensive fuels for heating and traveling. U.S. News and World Report has profiles of 1000 places for retirement, and "Best Places to Retire" according to a variety of criteria. Go to http://money.usnews.com/money/retirement/. This site also includes an excellent search feature by state by housing prices, plus a wealth of useful retirement information.

Most Affordable Cities to Buy a House

CNNMoney.com (www.cnnmoney.com) determined that the most affordable city to buy a house in 2010 is Indianapolis, IN, where median home prices last year were $106,000. Other cities include Detroit, MI ($86,000); Dayton, OH ($106,400); Youngstown, OH ($76,000); and Akron, OH ($100,000).

For those of you who dread the thought of cold winters, there has never been a better time to buy a retirement home in the Sunbelt or west. They are practically giving away condos in Florida. Ditto for Las Vegas – for both homes and condos. Arizona is another distress area. High foreclosure areas of sunny California offer outstanding homes in the $100,000 to $150,000 range. You can pick up nice homes in good neighborhoods at bargain prices with low interest rate financing.

Useful tools to locate retirement home candidates in another location are:

- Trulia Real Estate Search (www.trulia.com) – Comprehensive free tool for those searching for homes to buy or rent throughout the U.S. Plenty of useful advice too.

- Zillow (www.zillow.com) – Similar to Trulia. Offers free guess at home values based on surrounding comps and assessor data, a useful tool to get a ballpark valuation of your own home if you are thinking of selling.

- SocialServe (www.socialserve.com) – Offers listings for "affordable" housing and rentals. Provides free information by cities within states. More rental than housing data, but an excellent site for researching housing possibilities, especially if you are looking for a low-cost rental.

- RealtyTrac (www.realtytrac.com) – Good place to start if you are thinking about buying a foreclosure in another city. Lots of information, foreclosure listings and advice. Requires subscription but you can try it for free. You should also review Foreclosure.com (www.foreclosure.com).

Chapter 11 – Stretch your Dollars by Retiring Abroad

Thousands of Baby Boomers have retired abroad to stretch their retirement dollars. Every Boomer should give this option careful consideration. Moving to another country where the cost of living is lower offers substantial benefits for those without a large financial nest egg. In many countries, life on a small retirement income can be good...very good.

For example, what if you could retire to an area where a relaxing lifestyle can be enjoyed for just $1,200 monthly, and you can live well (with maids and gardeners) for, say, $2,500 monthly? Interested?

American enclaves exist for those who are afraid of cultural shock and language barriers. Health insurance and medical facilities are typically good. Financial matters are easily handled – Social Security benefits can be received by mail or direct deposit into a U.S. or foreign bank for American citizens. Internet and phone service are uninterrupted. Skype offers low-cost face-to-face conversations over the Internet. Climate and scenery are outstanding. Recreational activities are readily available. Safety is not a major concern - crime is typically less than in major U.S. cities. And you are just a plane ride away from family and friends in the United States.

Retiring abroad has been a quiet Boomer trend that is now picking up strong momentum. The number of Americans retiring abroad is expected to double in the next ten years. A good friend of mine who recently retired to Panama expressed his reasons for leaving the U.S.:

> *I cannot afford to retire in the US, mainly due to the high cost of medical insurance (until the age of 65), cost of property ownership, and so on. The choice of Central America, besides a terrific weather pattern, is enjoying affordable property values, affordable medical insurance/procedures, and inexpensive food prices. Being in the tropics, clothing costs are limited, and there are no heating bills. Air conditioning may be more comfortable but is not required in most areas. I love it here!*

A leading online community, Boomers Abroad (www.boomerabroad.com), amplifies these feelings and provides considerable insight and information for those considering the option of retiring abroad:

The number of Americans and Canadians living abroad has steadily grown over the past decade and it is expected to more than double within the next 10 years. Millions of Baby Boomers are discovering the affordable real estate, great quality of life and investment opportunities available abroad. Cold weather, high cost of living, health care costs and other issues are leading many to live and invest abroad.

It takes an adventuresome personality to move abroad. There are lots of considerations, but even on a low, fixed income it is possible to comfortably retire in a lifestyle that cannot be achieved here in the U.S.

A few words of caution. Retiring abroad requires upfront research, onsite investigation, and a lot of planning. For example, it is advisable to live in your selected location for a period of time before making a final decision to retire there. And if you are serious about retiring abroad, one should be prepared to learn the local language to fully benefit from the experience. There is also a cultural adjustment which requires an open mind and willingness to adapt to local ways. Otherwise, you will experience considerable frustration – "Type A" people, for example, may blow a gasket when they discover the inherent delays involved in obtaining simple permits or documents in Latin American countries. No matter where you retire abroad, it is going to be different than living in the U.S. If you are not prepared to accept that, retiring in another country is probably not your best choice.

Medicare is not applicable outside of the U.S, although you can always return to the U.S. for major health treatment, if necessary). So you will need to purchase a healthcare insurance policy if you retire outside the country. Fortunately, low-cost insurance and quality healthcare at much lower prices is readily available outside America.

It is also advisable to retain a U.S. address for banks, bills and other financial reasons. If you retire abroad, keep the majority of your liquid assets in the U.S. rather than a foreign bank to avoid any local currency devaluations and the danger that they might be uninsured.

For those who want an arm-chair experience of what is involved in retiring abroad, I strongly recommend purchasing *"How to Retire Overseas"* by Kathleen Peddicord, a true expert on the subject who has actually retired abroad. You can find her book on Amazon.

Excellent online resources you should explore are:

- International Living (www.internationalliving.com) – A huge site with lots of resources. They offer a free report: "The World's Top 10 Retirement Havens."

- Live and Invest Overseas (www.liveandinvestoverseas.com) – Considerable first-hand information and free reports. Offers free examples of living budgets by country.

- AARP (www.aarp.org) – Great articles and discussions on retiring abroad. Be sure to read, *"Best Places to Retire Abroad."*

- Boomers Abroad (www.Boomersabroad.com) – A free online community of Baby Boomers who have actually retired abroad or are thinking about it. Helpful information - You can compare Countries. You can compare Cities within a country and neighborhoods within a City.

- Expat Forum (www.expatforum.com) - The largest community of expatriates on the Internet, with close to 60,000 members.

- ExpatExchange (www.expatexchange.com) - Helps expats navigate international relocation and the phases of culture shock. Offers hundreds of reports from expatriates living abroad, expatriate resources and articles, international jobs, international real estate, travel warnings and more.

While there are many countries attracting Baby Boomers as retirement havens, most that likely fit your budget lie south of the border. A brief overview of these major retirement destinations is presented below.

Argentina

- Pro: Safe country for Boomers. Buenos Aires is a cosmopolitan city where real estate bargains can still be found. English widely spoken. Condo rentals start at $500 monthly. Good healthcare. Warm climate on coast, rest is much like the U.S. $2,000 monthly income said to be required to live a nice retirement.

- Con: Steep inflation and government bureaucracy.

Belize

- <u>Pro</u>: Central American paradise. Official language is English. Qualified Retired Persons program provides benefits and fast track to residency status. Live comfortably on $18,000 annually. U.S. dollar accepted. Rentals from $250-$500 monthly; houses from $75,000. Easy access to Mexico resort areas. Basic healthcare.

- <u>Con</u>: Hot and humid. Located in hurricane belt.

Brazil

- <u>Pro</u>: Cost of living is about half of U.S., but it is a modern country. Strong economy, stable government and good infrastructure along Atlantic coast. Good food and healthcare system. Cooler climate to the south; tropical beaches. Retire comfortably on $2,000 monthly.

- <u>Con</u>: Danger of catching a tropical disease outside major cities. Extreme poverty in city slums. Higher prices in major tourist cities (like Rio de Janeiro).

Chile

- <u>Pro</u>: Offers a lifestyle close to what you would see in the U.S. with similar cost of living. Need $4,000-$5,000 monthly to live comfortably. Get by on less if you buy a home ($200,000+).

- <u>Con</u>: Not the cheapest option for Boomer retirees.

Costa Rica

- <u>Pro</u>: Lush island and retirement life; famous for ecotourism. About 50,000 Americans live there. Central Valley offers temperate climate and tropical humidity. More like living in U.S. – malls, etc. Live comfortably on $3,000+ monthly – houses start at $100,000; rents are $500-$1,000 monthly. Excellent healthcare (at 30-70 percent less cost than U.S.). Abundant outdoor activities and nightlife.

- <u>Con</u>: More expensive than other retirement choices; government red tape to satisfy residency requirements.

Dominican Republic

- Pro: Can buy new home below $100,000. Inexpensive living. Tropical weather; sunny beaches and temperate mountain climates. Excellent healthcare (including medical tourism). Extensive recreation, including first-rate golf courses.

- Con: Located in hurricane belt. Danger of exposure to some tropical diseases.

Ecuador

- Pro: Most affordable choice. Live comfortably for $15,000-$25,000 annually. Rents start below $500 in Cuenca. Tropical along coast, becoming cooler inland at higher elevations. Buy beachfront condos for under $80,000. Lots of outdoor activities; nice beaches.

- Con: Limited healthcare, political instability, and crime.

El Salvador

- Pro: San Salvador is an overlooked city – a great place to retire; cosmopolitan. Beautiful beaches. Less humidity than some Central American countries – tropical on coast; temperate in highlands. Currency based on U.S. dollar. Can legally own land. Affordable – houses rent for $300-700 monthly. Overall, cost of living in cities is about one-third less than New York City.

- Con: Poor country. Personal safety is an issue in some areas. Densely populated. Major earthquake every 20 years. Hot water not available everywhere. Ability to speak basic Spanish is important.

Mexico

- Pro: Number 1 destination for retirees; easy access to U.S. Thriving expat communities (about 50,000 U.S. and Canadians) in Lake Chapala, near Guadalajara; San Miguel de Allende, in Guanajuato; Baja California; and Cancun, in the Yucatan. Real estate bargains. Temperate winters; hot and humid summers. Live comfortably on $1,000-$2,000 monthly. Rentals start around $800 monthly; home prices runs from $90,000 on up and financing is available. Excellent, inexpensive medical care. Import household goods tax-free.

- Con: Drug cartel wars in border towns, but most of country is relatively safe. Frustrating bureaucracies.

Nicaragua

- Pro: Poor country where the dollar goes a long way. Live comfortably on $18,000 annually (in some cases, cost of living is up to 60 percent less than in U.S.). Estimated 10,000 Americans live there. Beautiful beaches, mountains and scenery. Housing costs are $100,000-$200,000; rents run from $500-$1,500 monthly. Generally warm temperatures, with rainy summers. Great outdoor activities (surfing, sunning, hiking, arts, etc.). Tax incentives to lure U.S. retirees. Stable, safe country.

- Con: Healthcare outside major cities is basic; may have to go to Managua or major city for hospital care.

Panama

- Pro: Good choice for those that want it all on a budget. Hot beach towns; cool mountain villages. Excellent night life in Panama City. Expat communities with recreational facilities. Pensionado program for foreign retirees with guaranteed pension or Social Security income that offers property tax exemptions for new construction, a 1 percent mortgage reduction for a primary residence, and even 20-50 percent discounts on nearly everything to attract U.S. retirees. New home buyers don't have to pay taxes for up to 20 years. Live comfortably on $20,000 per year. Housing from $175,000; monthly rents from $600. Excellent healthcare facilities.

- <u>Con</u>: Flights to U.S. are centralized out of Panama City (to Miami).

Peru

- <u>Pro</u>: Reasonable cost of living. Can pick up a nice condo for around $30,000. Lots of outdoor activities and history to explore. Climate similar to southern California. Good inexpensive medical services in major cities. Rent homes starting around $400 monthly. Live comfortably on $20,000 annually.

- <u>Con</u>: Political instability. Personal safety is an issue.

Puerto Rico

- <u>Pro</u>: U.S. Protectorate. Vibrant society. Beautiful beaches. Modern. Homes cost generally less than in the U.S., but are more expensive than other areas in the Caribbean and Latin America.

- <u>Con</u>: High homicide rate. Can be expensive. Crowded, with high poverty rate. Must learn Spanish to fit in.

Uruguay

- <u>Pro</u>: Laid-back country. Montevideo resembles an old European city. In spite of the fact that the place is far from being urbanized, there are a lot of great restaurants and shops to visit. Need minimum of $18,000 annually to retire comfortably in one of the major cities.

- <u>Con</u>: May have to go back to U.S. to handle major medical issues. Knowing Spanish is highly suggested.

Some may ask about retiring to Canada. Its closeness to the U.S. in terms of culture and geography offers several advantages. Health care and living standards are among the highest in the world. However, if you are on a limited budget, the cost of living there is equal to or greater than that of living in the U.S. And you better love snow…

Chapter 12 – Reducing Everyday Expenses without Sacrificing your Lifestyle Quality

Reducing expenses is critical for most Baby Boomers who, because of job loss or otherwise, are on the verge of retiring. Don't expect to live like you did when you were employed. If your retirement is voluntary, you are exchanging a paycheck for freedom and control over your time - it is worth it! If your job went away, it is a necessity. Fortunately, there are several easy steps you can take to dramatically cut your expenses while still living comfortably.

Simply eliminating impulse buying can result in significant savings. Avoid use of credit cards, don't carry a lot of cash, rent rather than buy when feasible (e.g., rent a DVD for $3 instead of buying it for $20), and learn to stick to a budget. In an era of rising energy and food costs, retiring Boomers on a fixed or limited income must give high priority to overcoming wasteful spending habits and learning to stretch their dollars.

Fortunately, this is not as hard as it seems. Just the process of creating a monthly budget creates a mental alert system that curbs impulse buying. There are also tools and alternatives that support spending reductions without endangering the quality of your retirement. This chapter introduces these and hopefully engenders a new attitude that transforms your retirement lifestyle.

Below are some simple changes you can make in your everyday spending to stretch your retirement dollars. These do not dramatically affect the quality of your lifestyle. Essentially, it is just a matter of doing things differently so that you can enjoy a comfortable retirement within your financial means.

Revamp your Phone Service

You can easily save $40 to-$100 or more monthly by revamping your phone service.

Landline phone service is expensive and increasingly non-competitive. Retiring Baby Boomers should consider just using mobile phones or switching to Voice-Over-Internet-Protocol (VoIP), which typically offers unlimited worldwide calling for a low monthly charge. If you are running a business out of your home, you can easily switch to an inexpensive online fax service to eliminate a dedicated line.

Look at your mobile phone plan. Are you paying for a lot of "bells and whistles" that are rarely used? Does your carrier offer a less expensive plan for just the essentials? Is there another carrier with a better plan that suits your needs? Also, many carriers offer free calls when placed to someone using the same carrier – a possible reason to settle on one carrier among far-flung family members. Others offer alternative plans to the major carriers that are lower priced and more flexible. Most carriers also offer pre-paid plans which can help you budget your mobile phone calls by limiting the number of minutes to an acceptable level.

Learn to use Skype (www.skype.com) for face-to-face VoIP conversations using your laptop and a USB headset. Skype-to-Skype calls are free, and calls to landline and mobile phones are as cheap as $1.2 cents per minute!

Another VoIP provider, Vonage (www.vonage.com), allows use of your existing home phones (and phone number) while also offering considerable savings. For $26 monthly, you get what most phone companies may charge $55-$70 for. There are no annual contracts. Vonage is an especially good alternative for those who make a lot of international calls.

The major drawback with Skype and Vonage VoIP solutions is that if you lose power to your home, you lose your phone service. So it pays to retain your mobile phone service too while cutting back on its usage.

Cut Utility Costs

You can significantly reduce your utility expenses by instilling a few conservation habits:

- Lower the thermostat in winter and put it higher in the summer. Cut off heat or air conditioning to unused rooms by closing the air duct vents. Avoid using air conditioning whenever possible. Turn off (or lower) thermostat settings when not at home. Use fans whenever practical to reduce air conditioning bills. Ceiling fans help to circulate air year-round.

- Get rid of the second refrigerator in the garage. This can lower electricity bills by as much as 25 percent!

- Shut off lights as you leave a room. Turn of your PC and TV's when not in use.

- Fix leaky faucets. Caulk windows and seal drafty doors.

- Install water-saving kits in toilet cisterns.

- Reduce use of hot water. Save laundry until you have a full load. Do washing and rinsing in cold water as much as possible. Take shorter showers and turn off the water when soaping yourself up. Turn off the water when brushing your teeth.

- Buy Energy Star appliances when replacing a range, washer/dryer, refrigerator, dishwasher or trash compactor.

- Many utility companies will allow you to be billed even amounts based on your recent year-round billing. Doing this after implementing the above suggestions for a year will help you to plan expenses better.

- Take advantage of any senior discounts or programs offered by your local utility companies.

If you are willing to make an investment, switching to solar power will dramatically reduce your energy bill and perhaps generate an income by selling excess power to utility companies. There are also companies with new products that reduce your home electrical usage, prolong the life of appliances and provide home surge protection, yielding up to 30 percent savings on your electrical bill. KVAR (www.kvarexpress.com) is a leader in this field, offering a home unit for about $550 (installed).

Accomplishing these simple tasks and adhering to energy-saving habits can reduce your electric and/or gas bills by 30-to-50 percent monthly!

Clip Coupons and Shop Sales

Coupons are your friend. So are sales. When you are going shopping, search for applicable coupons or sales online and in the paper. Buy store brand consumables in bulk. With a little effort, you can experience immediate savings that really add up. Here are some websites that offer free coupons for a variety of shopping needs:

- Coupons.com (www.coupons.com) – Popular site that offers free coupons for a variety of products and services. Also sells discount coupons at significant savings. Must register for free account. Can receive email alerts.

- Coupon Cabin (www.couponcabin.com) – Over 148,000 free coupons and deals for over 3,000 stores. Search by store and category for just about everything you can imagine, from airline tickets to groceries to clothes. The average shopper spends 80 seconds on their site and saves $19 per order. Ability to set up email alerts.

- Smart Source (www.smartsource.com) - Good place to get printable grocery coupons by product; usable in all stores. Receive email alerts.

- Coupon Shack (www.couponshack.com) – Discount coupons for products and services, as well as groceries. Regularly offer "hot deals." Email alerts also available.

- Coupon Mom (www.couponmom.com) – Focused on coupons intended to reducing your grocery bill, drugstore costs and restaurant expenditures. Must create a free account to gain access. Ability to search for deals by state. Sign up for email alerts. Offers a virtual coupon organizer.

- RetailMeNot.com (www.retailmenot.com) - Helps you find coupon discounts for more than 65,000 online merchants and stores, including groceries. Just enter a domain name, store name or search by subject. Register for free online community to access tips and advice.

Online auctions, such as eBay (www.ebay.com), are also a good place to buy merchandise way below retail value. Honesty.com (www.honesty.com) finds bargains on eBay and you can use this site to set your own prices if you want to sell something on eBay.

Reduce your Home Entertainment Costs

According to Entertainment Trends in America, the current per capita spending on entertainment in the United States is $160 per month, with most of that devoted to television and internet services. In today's world, the cost of home entertainment, including Internet services, consumes more and more of our budget. It is like a sleeping monster that you realize one day has gotten out of hand. This monster can be tamed, however, by consolidating services and using innovative technology to reduce costs without sacrificing quality.

An easy way to cut costs is to consolidate your phone, TV and internet services under a single carrier. Economies of scale will give you access to special rates and promotions offered by the major carriers, such as Verizon, AT&T and Sprint.

Where these services get you is on packaged charges for optional TV or cable channels. And this is an area where you can really save by taking advantage of free online shows and services. Also, inexpensive technologies now exist which allow you to target only the movies you want to see, avoiding packaged pricing pushed by the carriers.

First, most of the major networks – CBS, ABC and NBC - offer online newscasts and the ability to view previously aired shows, sports and other programs over the Internet. You can watch some of these by going directly to their websites. Other free websites offer not only current network shows but also the ability to download older series and movies to your PC or laptop. If your laptop has an HDMI port, you can connect it directly to a high-definition TV for viewing as well. There are also inexpensive black boxes you can purchase that connect directly to your TV for downloading shows and movies from the Internet. All these approaches can save you a ton of money compared to cable company packages. Let's take a look at each:

Downloading TV Shows and Movies

For those of you who have not been exposed to downloading movies and TV shows over the Internet, it is a simple and effective process. This is now a mature technology and millions do it daily. Rather than provide tutorials and movie guides here, you are referred to the following articles by Wendy Boswell to learn how to do this and which sites offer downloads. Read these articles and you will know everything you need to know about using the Internet to watch TV and movies.

- Where can I Find Free Internet Movies? – An excellent introduction and guide to free movies. (http://websearch.about.com/od/freemovies/f/internetmovies.htm)

- Watch Movies Online – An outstanding directory of sites that offer free movie and TV show downloads. This site is well worth investigating. (http://websearch.about.com/od/freemovies/a/freemovies.htm)

- • The Top Ten Sites for Free Full-Length Movies – Great overview and links to the top ten sites for movies downloading and viewing on your PC or television. (**http://websearch.about.com/od/freemovies/tp/free-full-length-movies.htm**)

A nice feature is the ability to watch whole seasons of your favorite TV shows and movies. You can also burn them to DVD to create your own collection. Plus, they provide trailers for movies currently showing in theaters.

A word of caution – Some of the movie download sites require that you first download software to facilitate the process. This is OK, but be sure that you have up-to-date virus protection software, such as McAfee, to avoid contaminating your PC or laptop.

Many of the movie download sites offer an optional extended service where more movies and shows are available for streaming download not only to your PC or laptop, but Internet-based TVs (such as Vizio and those incorporating Google technology), black-box TV interfaces, Sony Blue-ray players, iPads, and mobile phones. These fees are typical under $10 monthly. *Netflix Watch Instantly* provides unlimited movies and TV episodes for a flat rate starting at $8.99 a month.

The downside of Internet entertainment viewing is that they don't always have the latest movies or TV show episodes, or may have just a few. However, their vast selection makes up for this. Also, there is little 1080 dpi high-definition content available on the Internet. But once you switch to Internet entertainment, you will quickly get hooked and understand why this medium will eventually displace brick and mortar theaters as well as providing a credible alternative to cable TV channel packaging.

TV-Internet Boxes

Newer flat-panel TV's have built-in Internet download capabilities. But if you have an older digital TV, don't worry. You can always upload a movie through the HDMI port or via Wi-Fi. A third alternative is to buy an inexpensive, worry-free black box which connects to your TV for directly downloading movies and shows from Internet sites. These media-streaming boxes sell for around $100 (occasionally less if you can find a special promotion).

A good video overview of the top 5 boxes can be viewed at http://revision3.com/tomstop5/toptvboxes. Time magazine recently covered this technology too in an article titled *"Here Come the New Internet-TV Boxes."* You can read this at http://www.time.com/time/business/article/0,8599,2021865,00.html. Suffice it to say that best solutions appear to be:

- Roku (www.roku.com) – Sells for $59.99 to $99.99. Pricier models include Wi-Fi and high-definition (1080 dpi) capabilities. Comes with remote control. Also sold by Amazon. In their own words, *"Watch movies and TV shows from Netflix, Hulu Plus or Amazon VOD, listen to music on Pandora, catch the latest ballgame, and more."*

- Apple TV (www.apple.com/appletv) – Retailing for $99, this may be the best solution for Apple fans. It streams *Netflix Watch Instantly* movies and shows. Apple also plans to offer movie rentals on its iTunes Store site.

- Logitech ReVu (www.logitech.com) – A powerful new solution based on Google TV technology that allows you to open multiple websites, social network sites and watch any videos on the Internet. It basically allows you to surf the Internet on your HDTV using Google search capabilities. Comes with a keyboard. Optional camera add-on allows you to make video calls using VoIP services such as Skype. You can download movies from Netflix and Amazon as well. Pricing starts around $229.

Satellite TV Services

Satellite TV services, such as DirectTV, the Dish Network, AT&T and Comcast, offer affordable alternatives to cable-based TV services. Monthly charges start around $30. They often offer introductory packages and usually provide a free dish and installation along with a free digital video recorder.

Satellite TV typically offers a wider variety of shows in the base package, but they also charge for the cable channels such as HBO and Showtime. Plus, they charge extra to watch recent movies (and sometimes even older movies). So the pricing difference between satellite and Cable TV is not a major factor, depending upon viewer preferences. You should compare the two to determine which offers the best package at the lowest price that best suits your needs.

There are some downsides, however. Satellite TV can experience interference from heavy snow or rain. Also, a south-facing location is required on which to mount the satellite dish. Moreover, you will likely need a separate Internet service provider.

FREE Movies

Did you know that most libraries offer free DVDs for check-out? You can now view your favorite movies and recent releases simply by taking a trip to your local library. Some libraries even have online sites where movies and documentaries can be downloaded for instant viewing on your PC, laptop or TV.

Cheap DVD Rentals

Redbox movie rentals (www.redbox.com) only charges $1.09 for viewing brand new movie releases. Their ubiquitous dispensers are located in supermarkets, drugstore, gas stations...just about everywhere. All you need is a credit or debit card to create an account and DVDs can be returned to any Redbox unit. They even email you information on upcoming new releases and you can reserve movies by Redbox location using their Internet site. It's simple and it works. Sure beats paying $5 to watch new movie releases through a cable or satellite dish company!

Cut Back on "Nice to Haves"

If you look around, you will probably see many costs that are not essential and therefore are ripe candidates to be cut. Some "extras" to consider dispensing with are:

- Bottled water (buy a filter for your kitchen faucet if you have water quality concerns).

- Premium cable channels (do you really need 800 channels?); cable boxes (and TVs) in just about every room.

- Magazine, newspaper and newsletter subscriptions.

Trim Insurance Costs

Selecting higher deductibles (and foregoing collision insurance on older cars) on auto and home protection policies can save hundreds of dollars annually. Ditto for consolidating all your policies – home, life and car – under a single carrier. And did you know that the higher your credit score, the lower your auto insurance premiums are? Yep, good credit equals fewer accidents.

If you are reading this book, you should definitely be looking at term life insurance compared to whole life insurance. You save money and get more service, but forego a cash-out value. The latter has little meaning to cash-strapped older Boomers. Shop around - term life insurance is affordable and widely available even for people in their sixties. Term4Sale (www.term4sale.com) is a good site for comparing term life insurance policies from different insurers. Be advised that rates increase considerably the older you become, so it's best to lock in a policy at an earlier age. Some organizations, such as AARP (www.aarp.org), offer "no physical" policies, but for lower amounts.

Perform Common Household Repairs and Upgrades Yourself

Baby Boomers can save a ton of money simply by learning how to perform common household repairs (leaky faucets, changing filters, faulty electrical switches, etc.) themselves. There are several online sites that present step-by-step instructions with photos to assist you.

This is also true for many household upgrades. You can do painting yourself and learn to tile bathrooms and counters, replace windows, install a garbage disposal, or lay flooring. Again, a multitude of Internet sites exist with "how to" instructions, and many neighborhood suppliers like Home Depot hold free regularly scheduled classes on these subjects.

Reduce Car Expenses

Car expenses consume a large part of our income. First, there's the cost of purchasing an automobile, then licensing, insurance, parking and regular maintenance, not to mention the skyrocketing cost of gasoline. Add it all up and it is a big chunk of money. One rule of thumb is that your total car expense should not exceed 20 percent of your household (after tax) income.

There are many ways for Baby Boomers to reduce their car expenses, and most of them are easy to implement. A good article offering useful advice is *10 Cheap Ways to Care for your Car*, which can be read at (www.smartmoney.com/spending/autos/10-cheap-ways-to-care-for-your-car/?cid=1231).

Replacing your Car

Buying a new car will dent your budget. Used cars cost considerably less. Since new cars dramatically depreciate in value during the first two years, you can get a "broken in" automobile that is still under warranty at up to a 50 percent savings! Save more money by looking for smaller, more fuel-efficient cars.

Here are some reputable Websites that can help you determine how much to pay for a new or used car, and assist you in finding a good, reliable used car:

- AutoWeb (www.autoweb.com) – Offers a ton of useful information and tools for researching new and used cars.

- Edmunds (www.edmunds.com) - Provides *True Market Value* pricing, unbiased car reviews, ratings, and expert advice to help you get a fair deal.

- Kelly Blue Book (www.kbb.com) – Current prices for new and used car trade-in values.

- CarMax (www.carmax.com) - Excellent online source for pricing, selling and buying used cars with a warranty.

Cut your Pet Care Costs

Pets are our surrogate children. They are important family members. But feeding and caring for them can be as expensive as raising a child. Here are some ways to cut pet care costs:

- Order discount food and medicine from online sites. These also provide free advice on training, nutrition and health issues. PetCareRX (www.petcarerx.com) is a good site to review.

- Review your local paper to see when animal shelters, humane societies or veterinarians are offering special clinics to save on vaccinations and neutering.

- Buy toys and chewies in bulk.

- Learn how to trim your pet's hair cut nails and brush their teeth.

- Make your own pet food by mixing low-priced market food (chicken, rice, pasta, vegetables, etc.). NoCans (www.nocans.com) and SimplyPets.com (www.simplypets.com) are two sites that offer pet food recipes.

- Learn how to treat your dog or cat for common ailments to save a bundle on vet bills. See The Web Pet Doctor (www.thewebpetdr.com) for a good example of online information.

Chapter 13 - Take Advantage of Inexpensive Travel

The Baby Boomer generation loves to travel. Maybe you envision traveling during your retirement years, but doubt that this is possible because you belong to the two-thirds of Baby Boomers retiring on a limited income.

Well, you won't be taking exotic cruises, but you certainly can travel and enjoy yourself. Domestic travel is affordable, and (with a little research) traveling abroad on a budget is still possible.

Inexpensive Domestic Travel

With rising gas prices, the cost of car travel to anywhere except local destinations is fast becoming prohibitive. We recommend traveling by train (Amtrak or other local train service) or bus. Try a short trip first to see if this is for you. You may be surprised at how enjoyable traveling by mass transit can be.

Low-Cost Local Vacations

Taking a local vacation is an inexpensive way to relax and enjoy yourself. With a little ingenuity, Baby Boomers on fixed incomes can stretch their dollars to partake of local delights. For example, stay a week at the beach during the off season when motel/hotel rates are much lower, or rent a home in the mountains or at the beach during the off season. Go to Las Vegas, where low-cost packages can always be found. Camping, timeshares and home swapping are just a few ways to enjoy an inexpensive vacation.

Do an Internet search to find good deals for the vacation you are seeking. Don't forget to use your AARP membership or ask for a senior discount to get even lower rates.

Low Cost Airfare

There are several Websites dedicated to identifying the lowest cost airfare to a destination of your choice. Many support centralized searches of such popular sites as Orbitz, Travelocity and Priceline. One site to look at is www.BookingBuddy.com. Some (such as www.BestFares.com) are membership based, but cover everything from vacation packages to cruises.

Traveling Abroad on a Budget

With the depreciated dollar and increased airfares, foreign travel is expensive for Baby Boomers on a fixed income. Nonetheless, economical vacations (e.g., one-to-two weeks under $3,000 with travel, transportation, meals and lodging included) can still be found if you shop around. Relaxing, affordable travel vacations to some parts of the world, such as Latin America, are also available.

CafeBabyBoomers.com (www.cafeBabyBoomers.com) has a multitude of useful articles that can help you find affordable travel vacations. Check under "Travel/Leisure." BabyBoomerTrips.com (www.Babyboomertrips.com) is another good place to find travel bargains. And don't forget to visit the AARP site (www.aarp.org) for tips and special values. Boomeropia (www.boomeropia.com) is also a Baby Boomer travel site where you can find interesting trips at affordable prices.

Affordable Baby Boomer Cruises

If you enjoy visiting foreign ports, dancing, live music, dining, gambling, etc., then an ocean cruise may be the ideal vacation for you. Typically, everything is included in the price tag, so you don't have to worry about extra costs or arranging hotel, dining, entertainment, and other activities. But be careful of the "booze bill." That's where cruise outfits make their money.

Short Caribbean or Baja California cruises are especially affordable. Boomers 55 and older can often get discounts. Going on a cruise during the off season can result in some real bargains! Search for "Cheap Cruises" in Google or Yahoo.

Join Clubs

There are many inexpensive clubs that offer economical travel and recreation. The Sierra Club (www.sierraclub.org) is a great option for those that enjoy hiking, outdoor activities and social gatherings. Local bicycling clubs also abound. Another fun thing is to join a brewer's club to learn how to make beer and wine at home, plus you get to drink a lot of free booze at meetings and social events. Just search the Internet for a club centered around your interests – you'll be surprised at how plentiful they are.

Chapter 14 –Reducing Healthcare Costs for Those Under 65

For older Baby Boomers not yet on Medicare, healthcare is a major expense. Studies show that it can consume 5-to-10 percent of after-tax income for Boomers in the 50-64 year old age bracket. Any dent you can make in healthcare expenditures will boost spendable income. Fortunately, healthcare insurance and discount programs for older Boomers are available. It is still a challenge, but there are options and strategies which can save you money.

Shop Health Insurance

Seeking affordable Healthcare insurance for Baby Boomers is a particularly difficult undertaking for those who are not covered by a pension plan and too young to qualify for Medicare (65). It is a huge expensive void.

If you are a Baby Boomer whose income is under $1,000 monthly, you might just want to forego health insurance altogether and seek to qualify for a state-run program. Barring that, if you are in good health, consider foregoing healthcare insurance and hope that you stay well and do not suffer an illness or accident before you qualify for Medicare at age 65. Chances are, if something happens, there is a fund somewhere that would pick up all or a large portion of the costs (although medical bills may first consume whatever assets you have).

For the rest of older Baby Boomers, getting individual or family healthcare insurance is costly, as much as $2,000 or more monthly depending on pre-existing conditions. Just getting a quote is typically an extensive process, requiring completing comprehensive online forms which ask such personal questions as "Have you ever smoked marijuana?" Of course, no Baby Boomers have.

There are some things you can do to minimize your health insurance costs. If you and your family are in general good health, consider starting a Health Savings Account (HSA). This is a personal account that lets Baby Boomers pay for qualified medical expenses with tax-advantaged funds. You or an eligible family member make contributions to your HSA tax-free, and those dollars earn interest tax-free. Then, when you make withdrawals from your account to pay for qualified health care expenses, they are tax-free too.

Do not rush into a healthcare policy. Some things to look for when you are evaluating health insurance programs are:

- What the out-of-pocket expenses are for co-pays and deductibles for doctor visits and prescriptions.

- Does the hospitalization portion includes the room and board and incidentals, and whether the surgical coverage includes the surgeon's fee as well as the procedure.

- AARP Essential Premier Health Insurance, insured by Aetna Life Insurance Company (Aetna), is custom-designed exclusively for AARP members 50-64 and their dependents. These plans are flexible for people who are retired, looking into early retirement, coming off of COBRA, self-employed or seeking coverage for dependents.

Bear in mind that although health insurance is expensive, there are some major benefits that cannot be discounted:

- Your co-pay is based on significantly reduced rates negotiated by the insurance company. If you had to pay the full amount yourself, it would be considerably higher.

- Without health insurance, an accident or serious illness could wipe out all your assets.

The new healthcare law will help Boomers in the future:

- The uninsured and self-employed would be able to purchase insurance through state-based exchanges with subsidies available to individuals and families with income between the 133 percent and 400 percent of poverty level ($22,050 for a family of four).

- Starting in 2014, insurance companies won't be able to turn away people with pre-existing conditions, or to charge sick people higher premiums.

- Separate exchanges will be created for small businesses to purchase coverage — effective 2014.

Discount Healthcare

Rather than purchasing insurance, a low-cost alternative is to join a healthcare discount program. These typically offer a discount of 10-to-60 percent for health services at participating doctors nationwide. Instead of paying hundreds of dollars each month for healthcare insurance, you would typically pay less than $100 monthly to join a program. There is no physical or qualification process involved.

This is a possible solution for those who cannot afford health insurance and/or are in relatively good health. Just make sure there is a medical provider in your area that will take your discount card before signing up for any plan! Learn more about discount healthcare programs at the Consumer Health Alliance before buying into any plan (www.consumerhealthalliance.com).

One discount healthcare solution to review is KeyLife Benefits, which offers wellness services through nationwide health service providers. Key Life membership also provides discounted legal, dining, hearing, vision and roadside assistance services.

Cutting your Prescription Costs

For those who do not yet qualify for Medicare, drug prescriptions can be a major cost item. Actions you can take to reduce prescription costs are:

- Ask your doctor to redirect you to a generic version(s) of your drug(s).

- Tell your doctor that you cannot afford the prescribed drug(s). They usually have free samples from pharmaceutical companies that they can give you.

- If you are a veteran, go to the VA to get your prescriptions. Honorably-discharged veterans can get many prescription drugs for $8 monthly through the VA Health Care System (877-222-8387; www.va.gov).

- Generally, if you earn less in a year than $39,200 for single people or $52,800 for couples, you may qualify for free prescription drugs. Learn more at the Free Medicine Foundation (www.freemedicinefoundation.com).

- AARP members get discounts on prescriptions, vision and hearing products at leading retail outlets (www.aarp.org).

- Get a free True Care card (www.truerxdiscount.com) that provides nationwide discounts of up to 60% on drugs purchased at Rite-Aid, Walgreens or Target.

- Pharmaceutical companies patient assistance programs will provide free drugs to families making as much as $40,000 - $70,000 annually. For details, go to the pharmaceutical company's Website or call their 800 number.

Even if you already have independent healthcare insurance, you may be able to save money by canceling the prescription drug part of your policy and taking advantage of one of the above programs or tactics.

Low-Cost Dental Plans

Seeing a dentist when you are a Baby Boomer on a fixed or limited income can be expensive. The good news is that there are inexpensive dental plans you can join for just a few dollars monthly. While they don't cover all the dental costs, they do provide substantial discounts on dental services. Discount dental plans have quickly become an attractive alternative to costly dental insurance.

Generally speaking, these dental plans entitle you to a discount on dental services. Baby Boomers can avail themselves of these discounts at any registered dentist. Dental discounts can cover all dental problems whether it is pre-existing or not.

Joining a dental plan has several advantages for Baby Boomers on a fixed or limited income. They are affordable and there is no long application form. There are no health restrictions and they are quickly activated. The average cost is $90-$170 annually for an individual; $100-$200 annually for families.

Two sites to visit if you are interested in discount dental plans are:

- AARP Dental Insurance (www.deltadentalins.com/aarp/us/index.html) - AARP has a partnership with Delta Dental to provide inexpensive dental plan coverage for seniors. If you are an AARP member, this is the way to go. Their plans offer 50-100% discounts on dental procedures up to a maximum of $1,500 annually.

- Discount Dental Plans (www.dentalplans.com) - This site provides an excellent overview of all dental plans offered under their umbrella. It is a good place to acquaint yourself with what is available and get pricing comparisons. Unlike some others, this is a reputable operation with solid credentials.

The main catch to discount dental plans is that you have to use a dentist who accepts your plan. Also, you must pay the dentist for the balance (after discount) on the day of service (unless you personally make arrangements otherwise with your dentist).

Discount Vision Care

Vision care for Baby Boomers can be an expensive issue. But there are some programs that mitigate the cost to you:

- Join AARP (www.aarp.org), whose members save 30 percent on eyewear (exams, frames, lenses, and lens options) and up to 20 percent on contact lens.

- EyeMed Vision Care (http://portal.eyemedvisioncare.com) - Founded by LensCrafters, it offers affordable vision care insurance to individuals and small businesses.

Chapter 15 – Handling Parental Care Issues and Expenses

Baby Boomers becoming caregivers for one or both of their parents face a challenging and rewarding responsibility. If you are in this group, you belong to a fast growing segment of the Baby Boomer population. Parental care is difficult, but giving back support and love to your parents can create a special time that brings you closer.

Recognize that your roles are switching - you are becoming the parent as they hand over more responsibility and authority over their lives to you. The time will likely come when you have to make decisions for them. That is why you should:

- Make sure your parent(s) have a Living Will, so that their wishes can be carried out as they approach death (e.g., do not resuscitate or unnecessarily extend life by artificial means). Most hospitals will not let you make decisions for your parent(s) unless you are so appointed in a Living Will.

- As a related caregiver, you should have a notarized Power of Attorney that allows you to make decisions if your parent(s) are incapable of doing so. It is also a good idea to become a joint account holder on their bank accounts and investments. If your parents have a living trust, you should be named as successor trustee, so you can step in as financial manager if needed.

- Have a written list of all the medications your parent(s) use, including dosage. Know how to contact their primary care physician. Have copies of their insurance records. This is very important information for emergency room personnel and hospitals.

- Discuss funeral and internment wishes with your parent(s).

- In a tactful way, help your parent(s) sort through their belongings. Whom would they like to receive special items? What can be gotten rid of?

- Make sure your parent(s) have a written, witnessed Will to avoid the messy, expensive and lengthy probate process. Ideally, the primary caregiver should be the Executor of the Will. Quicken WillMaker is an easy, inexpensive way to prepare a legal Will while working directly with your parent(s). Attorneys often prepare Wills for an affordable fixed fee as well.

- Know where all important documents are.

Being a primary caregiver for your parent(s) can be expensive too. Likely, your parents have Social Security benefits and perhaps veteran benefits as well. Certainly, your parent(s) are receiving Medicare benefits. If your parent(s) are also financially solvent, their income and savings can also help to defray health expenses.

If your parent(s) require assisted living or nursing home services, costs can quickly spiral out of control. Inheritances and all your parents' assets are often consumed unless prior financial steps to protect them have been taken or they are one of the fortunate few having long-term care insurance.

It is important that you explore options to handle long-term care issues before it becomes necessary. Medicaid (https://www.cms.gov/MedicaidEligibility/) is often an answer if your parent(s) have few resources. Medicaid urges those with limited resources to apply:

Apply if you are aged (65 years old or older), blind, or disabled and have limited income and resources. Apply if you are terminally ill and want to get hospice services. Apply if you are aged, blind, or disabled; live in a nursing home; and have limited income and resources. Apply if you are aged, blind, or disabled and need nursing home care, but can stay at home with special community care services. Apply if you are eligible for Medicare and have limited income and resources.

Ask Medicare (http://www.medicare.gov/caregivers/) is a site that provides information about Medicare, health care services, caregiver assistance sites and personal caregiver anecdotes.

Income and resource guidelines must be satisfied to qualify your parent(s) for Medicaid. Rather than trying to comprehend these complex guidelines yourself, nursing homes, assisted living facilities and hospitals have trained staff that can help you and process the paperwork.

Need help? *Eldercare Locator* is a free service that puts you in touch with state, local and federal senior services organizations. They can provide meals, transportation, training and in-home professional services to assist you as a caregiver or to help your parent(s) continue to live independently in the community. You can find them on the Internet at (http://www.eldercare.gov/Eldercare.NET/Public/Index.aspx).

BenefitsCheckUp.org (www.benefitscheckup.org) is a free online service where Baby Boomers can identify and explore benefits to which they and their parent(s) are entitled. A service of the National Council on Aging, it covers local, state and federal programs.

Many Boomers whose parent(s) are still able to live on their own are doubling up these days to cover living expenses. Having your parent(s) move in with you (or vice versa) is one way ride out the recession while also being in a position to monitor their activities and provide assistance.

If you are a parental caregiver, you are not alone. Millions of Baby Boomers are in the same position. Do not be reluctant to reach out for help. There are plenty of available resources to assist you in making the caregiver role easier and provide guidance in dealing with financial issues. Take advantage of them to keep your retirement dreams alive.

Chapter 16 – Real World Examples

OK, let's incorporate what we have learned into a few real-world examples. These will help you to understand how the knowledge you've gained can benefit your personal situation. Of the five examples, you will likely find one that reflects your challenges.

Example 1 – Older Boomer Loses Job

John Smith, age 58, lost his $90,000 position as the Vice President of Human Relations at a large corporation two years ago. He has been unsuccessful in finding new employment and his unemployment benefits have run out. His wife, Margaret, works as a secretary and brings in $3,000 monthly. They had $250,000 in savings, but the recession and subsequent stock market plunge cut that in half so that only $125,000 remains. Their home was valued at $400,000. However, the current market value is just $150,000 and their two mortgages total $300,000. They have been in trouble for several months, having to dig into their savings just to cover mortgage payments, taxes and HOA fees totaling $2,100 monthly plus handling basic necessities.

They are in a downward spiral. Unless John and Margaret take action, their remaining savings will be consumed sustaining a property that is unlikely to return to its former value for five-to-ten years. They are throwing good money after bad.

John and Margaret first try to get a loan modification on their home, but the lenders turn them down. Likewise, the lenders deny them the right to do a short-sale because they have been making their mortgage payments and have savings that the lenders feel can continue to be used for that purpose.

In response, John and Margaret team with a Realtor who is a specialist in short sales. They immediately stop making house payments while the professional negotiates a short sale deal with the lenders based on their financial hardship. This process carries on for several months, during which John and Margaret save considerable money and seek new employment in an area of the country where jobs are coming back and they feel they would like to someday retire. In the interim, the major lender begins foreclosure on their property despite being in the midst of the short-sale process.

John and Margaret both secure employment in the area of their choice, not making as much money as previously enjoyed, but happy to have jobs. They rent a nice home and move to the new location. Meanwhile, the first lender eventually agrees to the short sale and a buyer is found. The second lender negotiates a $5,000 payment in return for not sending debt collectors after them. The matter is settled.

So, John and Margaret are now living in an area they like, both employed (with employer-provided health care insurance), and with their remaining savings intact. They plan to boost their employer-matched 401K contributions to prepare for retirement. Both, however, intend to work until they are 66 to receive higher Social Security benefits. And because of the successful short sale, they will be eligible to receive a loan within a few years which will allow them to buy a retirement home. The major downsides are that they have to deal with mortgage relief on their upcoming tax return for a portion of the forgiven balance on the second mortgage and wait out the time to repair their credit records.

Had the short-sale been unsuccessful, John and Margaret still had the options of possibly renting their home out, walking away from it or simply continuing to live there (payment free) until it went into foreclosure.

Fortunately, everything worked out for them. They were careful about timing their move to ensure they had secured employment and a rental home before damaging entries showed up in their credit reports. The main thing is that they salvaged their remaining savings. Otherwise, their retirement outlook would have been bleaker.

Example 2 – Boomers Forced into Retirement with Little Savings

Both Bill Jones and his wife, Alice, are 62. They have lived the good life, spending almost all of their ample income on a $500,000 home, cars, travel, toys and college for their kids.

Then the Great Recession hit. Within 12 months, both found themselves out of jobs with no employment prospects on the horizon. The only financial resources they have are unemployment compensation totaling $2,200 monthly and $30,000 savings in 401Ks.

Their home fell upside down in value – it is now appraised at just $250,000, but has a mortgage of $400,000 and monthly payments for principal, interest and taxes at $2,781. Moreover, they had run up $20,000 in credit card debt. They are in a world of hurt. Unless Bill and Alice became proactive, they will quickly lose what little savings are left and become homeless.

Because of the credit card debt, Bill and Alice meet with a qualified attorney to negotiate a livable payment plan. Ultimately, they decide to pursue a Chapter 13 bankruptcy to pay off their debts without starving in the process.

Their house situation is hopeless. They decide the best situation is to let it go into foreclosure. Fortunately, they live in a non-recourse state where the lender cannot come after them for the unpaid balance and there is no tax relief issue. Since there are so many foreclosures in their area, lenders are taking up to 18 months to complete the foreclosure process. Meanwhile, they have stopped making payments and are living in their home for free. The lender doesn't care because they are maintaining the landscaping and generally keeping the home value from further deteriorating.

Bill and Alice need more income, so they applying for their Social Security benefits now rather than waiting until their full retirement age. Between them, they receive $2,900 monthly in benefits (which is protected from creditors) as their unemployment compensation expires. Since both are in good health, they decide to purchase discount health and prescription policies rather than pay the large premiums demanded by full health care insurance carriers. They learn to embrace coupons and manage to reduce their living expenses. Consequently, they find they can live quite nicely within their means, albeit giving up luxury travel trips in favor of nearby recreation and visits with their kid's families.

Bill decides to leverage his architect credentials and work experience to become a consultant for architectural firms. He creates a website and markets himself online. Within a year, he is supplementing their income to the tune of $2,000 monthly just working part-time. Tax write-offs allow them to keep their net income below the Social Security earnings limit. Their monthly income has now grown to $4,900, so they expedite paying off their credit card debt.

After 18 months when the foreclosure process concludes, they have a healthy monthly income and their credit card debt has been cut in half. Now their main problem is where to live. During this time, they have decided they wish to retire close to their son's family in the Midwest. Since it makes no difference where Bill runs his home-based business, they move to Omaha where their son works. Rents and home prices are low there. They find a nice home to rent, using a larger upfront deposit to overcome qualms about their tarnished credit scores. Life has gone from disastrous to one with a positive outlook.

Years later, Bill has transitioned his business so that it provides mostly passive income and he now works just a few hours weekly. At age 70, their credit restored, they decide to retire in Florida, where a low-priced condo with low monthly payments had previously been acquired by their son to whom they reimbursed payments through "gifts." Their remaining savings provide a fund for emergencies. Both are now covered by Medicare. Life is good.

Alternatively, Bill and Alice could have just walked away from their upside-down home and resettled anywhere, having made advance arrangements for a roof over their heads while their credit scores were still good. Or, they could have lived quite well in Panama or another country south of the border.

Example 3 – Boomers Retiring on a Low Income after Losing their Home and Savings

Jim and Grace are both 63. They have worked at blue collar jobs all their adult lives and basically lived month-to-month. Because of the Great Recession, both lost their jobs, all but $10,000 of their savings, and their home was foreclosed. Their unemployment compensation is running out, but no jobs are in sight. In the very near future, they face living on the streets. They have to do something and do it quickly!

First, Jim and Grace each immediately apply to receive their Social Security benefits. Between them, they are eligible to receive $2,300 monthly. Now, they at least have some income to go with their meager savings.

After reading this book, Jim and Grace feel more upbeat about their prospects. They could retire to a co-housing project in Arizona or rent a mobile home in a senior's community in Texas. Fortunately, Jim and Grace have a friend, Ron, who retired to Panama. Ron invites them down for a visit. When they see how well he is living on an income of $1,600 monthly and learn about the incentives provided by the Panama government to attract U.S. retirees, they decide to take the plunge.

Flash-forward six months - Jim and Grace are now settled near their friend in Panama. They rent a two-bedroom home in the temperate mountains with a weekly gardener and maid. They are both learning Spanish and enjoying the benefits of low-cost healthcare, inexpensive food and travel, Internet access, the camaraderie of a growing expat community, and the friendliness of local residents. They use Internet TV to watch U.S. programs and catch the latest movies. Moreover, they are slowly building their savings with the money left over each month. What could have been a tight retirement has turned into a comfortable and exciting lifestyle.

Example 4 – Retiring Boomers Need to Supplement their Income

James and Martha, age 63, have lived in their home for twenty-five years and wish to retire there to be close to friends and family. His job disappeared two years ago and unemployment compensation has run out. Martha has occasionally worked but has mostly been a homemaker.

James has started a home-based multi-level marketing business that currently yields $300 monthly. They have consumed their savings just to get by over the last two years and are now concerned about how they are going to pay the bills every month.

Their one piece of good fortune is that they only owe $33,599 on their home which has a current market value of $200,000. They originally purchased the property for $100,000 and the monthly principal and interest payments are $665. They have worked hard to all but pay off their mortgage so they could be assured of having a roof over their heads during old age.

Even though Martha just worked off and on, she is still entitled to some Social Security benefits. So to generate a monthly income, they both apply to get their Social Security benefits, receiving a combined income of $1,700 monthly. They cut their health insurance benefits to the bone and apply the cost-reduction strategies outline in this book to trim living expenses. Now they scrape by each month on $2,000, but it's tight. It would be nice to have some extra income so they don't have to "cheat death" every month. They would also like to buy a "new" used car to replace their aging vehicle.

After reading about it on the AARP website, James and Martha decide to seek a reverse mortgage for their home. Working with an ethical broker, they acquire a reverse mortgage that provides them with an additional $317 monthly in income while allowing them to cease mortgage payments. Moreover, they can continue to live in their home for the rest of their lives. Without the house payments, the combined boost to their monthly spendable income is $972.

When they both turn 65, they become eligible for Medicare, which reduces their health care insurance and medical care costs, consequently further increasing their spendable income. James' MLM business has grown and now brings in $1,300 monthly. Their total monthly income has grown to $3,000, living expenses are minimal, they have no house payment and they are building an emergency savings fund. It is not how much you make, but how much you keep!

Example 5 – Make Lemonade Out of Lemons!

Jamie is a single 57 year old woman who works as administrative manager for a medical practice. Her annual income is $65,000. Five years ago, Jamie purchased a condo outside Phoenix, Arizona for $150,000. Today, neighboring condos in her complex are selling for $80,000.

Obviously, Jamie is not happy about her investment. She is currently paying $1,256 (principal and interest) plus $80 HOA fees monthly to live there ($1,336 total). If she could sell her property and just buy another condo in her complex, her monthly payments would go down by $586!

Jamie contacted the bank and tried to get her mortgage adjusted to fit today's values. No dice. She then inquired about a short-sale and they told her she doesn't qualify since she can obviously continue to make the monthly payments.

After digesting this book, Jamie got smart. First she aligned herself with a Realtor and a savvy mortgage broker. Turns out she could qualify to purchase a second home. Jamie subsequently bought a very nice, single family residence close to her daughter's home at a discounted price of $125,000. She borrowed the 10 percent down payment from her 401K to avoid early withdrawal penalties. With today's low interest rates, her monthly principal and interest payment is only $686, and there are no HOA fees.

Then Jamie let her Realtor, who specializes in short sales, negotiate with the bank about the condo. Jamie presented her age and upcoming retirement as a need to reduce house payments in order to live off her savings and anticipated income. Meanwhile, she quit making payments on the condo and moved to her new home. The bank eventually accepted her hardship explanation and approved the condo short sale. Within a year, the condo was sold. Since Jamie lives in a non-recourse state, the bank cannot come after her and (thanks to the federal government) there is no mortgage relief to declare on her taxes.

Sure, Jamie's credit score will be dinged for a few years, but that is repairable. Meanwhile, look at what she accomplished after being told by the bank to take a hike! First, she saved a large amount when she stopped making condo payments. Plus, Jamie now lives in a wonderful home while saving $650 monthly compared to her previous condo payment, a figure that will boost spendable income when she retires. This outcome verifies a motto I personally live by – "Never piss off a smart lady."

Chapter 17 – Now it is Up to You!

As you have by now discerned, your retirement options are for the most part determined by the income and savings you have to work with. Once you have estimated what your monthly income is likely to be, then the ballpark options for retiring while keeping a roof over your head tend to be:

Anticipated Monthly Retirement Income	Best Retirement Options
<$1,500	Take your Social Security benefits as soon as possible. Use medical and dental discount programs to cut insurance costs if you are not yet 65; use your VA prescription benefits if you are a veteran.
	Rent a mobile/manufactured home or apartment in a low-cost area of the country. Look at co-housing opportunities and properties in rural areas where a USDA loan is possible.
	Tap into local or state assistance programs available to you. Declaring bankruptcy may be an option. Consider retiring in Central or South America.
$1,500 - $3,000	Any of the above options, plus possibly renting a residence in a low-cost area of the country or south of the border. Veterans may be able to buy a retirement home with zero down at a bargain price in the southwest or Florida.
	For homeowners, consider a reverse mortgage or renting out your property. Dispose of your home through a short sale or foreclosure if it is upside-down on the mortgage. If you have equity and want to downsize, consider selling your home with carry-back financing.
	If you have a job or business, continue to work and build

Anticipated Monthly Retirement Income	Best Retirement Options
	retirement savings; delay taking Social Security benefits as long as possible. Otherwise, start a home-based business or work part-time. Drive down living expenses.
$3,000+	Any of the above, plus consider purchasing a retirement home in a low-cost area of the country or south of the border. Take advantage of today's low prices and interest rates to ensure a roof over your head during retirement.
	Accelerate savings if you are still working. Strategize how to maximize your Social Security benefits. Implement a home-based business, if necessary, to supplement your anticipated retirement income.

Regardless of which category your unique situation falls into, the cost reduction strategies and tools outlined herein are applicable. Every measure you can take to stretch your dollars will make your retirement more comfortable. Likewise, supplementing your retirement income with a home-based business or part-time employment can make a huge difference in your lifestyle.

Even if you are facing a scary situation at the moment, it is not hopeless. There are opportunities to overcome retirement obstacles as long as you open your mind to alternative strategies that allow you to comfortably live within your financial means.

Having digested this book, the next step is to develop a plan based on your unique situation. Start by identifying a reasonable vision, then set goals for your retirement. Next, figure how to achieve them. No matter how bleak things may look now, you have the power to overcome obstacles and craft a comfortable retirement.

You must become proactive! Research the ideas, programs and tools presented herein to flesh out details. Explore home-based businesses or part-time work to discover feasible opportunities. Once you have an achievable vision of what you want your retirement to look like, back out an action plan for getting there. Test your assumptions – are they practical or wishful thinking? Bounce ideas off family members and friends to get constructive feedback. If possible, find a knowledgeable mentor to guide you in this process.

Never give up hope. Brush discouragement aside. Other Boomers in your situation – and believe me, there are millions – have overcome the same challenges and succeeded. Your future is in your own hands. You have the tools and knowledge to create a comfortable, enjoyable retirement. This is an exciting undertaking. Have a good journey!

Chapter 18 – My Story

Like you, my wife and I are Baby Boomers. We too saw the cumulative savings of years of employment bleed away when the economy crumbled in 2008. Before I knew what was happening, half of our 401Ks disappeared. And then our home equity evaporated and we found ourselves upside-down on the mortgage. In a short period of time, our retirement plans went down the drain.

Fortunately, my wife and I were old enough to begin taking Social Security benefits, which became a life saver as the recession deepened. I also had been self-employed for several years. My work experience allowed me to create a home-based marketing consulting business which provided a steady income. In addition, I had launched several web-based operations that provide passive income. And I had self-published several "How to" books that are widely distributed. So although my wife no longer worked and the recession sliced into our income, we managed to survive.

Despite the recession, I begin to formulate plans for eventual retirement. Not that I intend to give up working until I'm older…much older. But the world had shifted under my feet, and if I wanted to survive without having to work full-time forever, I needed a plan. I had to re-group to get our shattered financial house in order.

I started to think outside the box and look at creative approaches to retirement. Countless hours were spent surfing the web and exploring alternatives. There were many discussions with industry analysts and fellow Boomers in the same situation. It took many months, but eventually paid off.

I came up with a plan, refined it, bounced it off knowledgeable friends and professionals, and then we started a careful step-by-step implementation in 2009.

First, I researched areas where I thought of retiring and settled on the community of Menifee just north of Temecula in Riverside County, California. It offers a sunny climate, nice homes, golf courses, shopping centers, entertainment and nearby outdoor recreation. We found a rental home in a community next to a lake and moved within a few months. Yet we're still close enough to visit friends in San Diego and take bike rides along the beach.

Meanwhile, I performed repairs and painted our San Diego condo. I couldn't sell it because it is $50,000 underwater. Instead, I rented it out at what is essentially a break-even scenario. This has allowed us to retain a high credit score. After about one year, the now seasoned rental is not a handicap when applying for a home loan. I got my VA Eligibility Certificate renewed, and we are currently purchasing a home in an ideal location in Menifee. We're buying a house at a heavily discounted price, several hundred thousand dollars less than it sold for just a few years ago. Moreover, with today's low interest rates, our monthly payments are going to be very affordable.

In other words, using the principles described in this book, we are making lemonade out of lemons. As older Boomers, we are surviving the largest upheaval of any group of people since the Great Depression. And not just surviving, but living a comfortable lifestyle with enjoyable experiences while looking forward to a secure future. And you can too. Develop your own plan and go for it! We did it – you can too.

About the Author

As a Baby Boomer himself, Al Kernek turned 62 just as the economic bubble began to burst and the Great Recession started to unfold. He and his family suffered all the emotional and financial consequences described within these pages, along with millions of older Boomers.

He writes from personal experience. This book is an outgrowth of the research conducted as Al formulated his own survival plan. Some of this work is presented in a Website he established to help older Baby Boomers deal with the effects of the Great Recession and the disastrous impact on their retirement plans. Visit www.BabyBoomerLifeboat.com for recent developments and new programs targeted to help Baby Boomers. Also check out his blog (http://BoomerMuse.BabyBoomerLifeboat.com) for discussion of current issues.

Al is a former Air Force officer and Vietnam veteran with over thirty years of hands-on marketing and management experience in both Fortune 1000 firms and entrepreneurial start-up companies. He has an extensive background in Internet marketing and business consulting.

His credentials include a bachelor's degree in mathematics, a master's degree in business management, plus many industry and company awards for outstanding achievement. He is also a licensed real estate broker in California.

Al has published two previous books which are widely available in retail and online outlets. One is for real estate agents interested in email newsletters. This can be found at http://www.RENewsletter.com, a Website dedicated to providing Internet marketing tools and services for Realtors. The other book is designed to help small business people and entrepreneurs seeking to market their business online. Both are written in plain English for non-techies. See www.SmallBizSmartMarketing.com for details.

Among Al's many interests are a passion for bike riding along the California coastline, skiing, good mystery and horror novels, charitable works and mentoring small businesses. He resides with his wife and an assortment of critters in Menifee, California. Please contact Al with any questions or comments at his business email: akernek@Babyboomerlifeboat.com. All comments are welcomed.